THE PRICE OF SUCCESS

Also by J. B. Phillips

Translations

1947 Letters to Young Churches
1952 The Gospels in Modern English
1955 The Young Church in Action
1956 St. Luke's Life of Christ
1957 The Book of Revelation
1958 The New Testament in Modern English
1963 Four Prophets
1972 The New Testament in Modern English, Revised Edition
1981 The Living Gospels of Jesus Christ (illustrated by works of
       the great Renaissance Masters)

Other writings

1952 Your God is Too Small*
1954 Plain Christianity
1954 Appointment With God
1954 When God Was Man
1956 New Testament Christianity
1956 The Church Under the Cross
1957 Is God at Home?*
1957 God With Us
1959 A Man Called Jesus*
1960 God Our Contemporary
1967 Ring of Truth*
1967 Ring of Truth, New Edition with correspondence
1976 Peter's Portrait of Jesus (a Commentary)

Anthologies

1960 Good News – Thoughts on God and Man
1961 The Christian Year
1974 Through the Year with J. B. Phillips
1978 The Newborn Christian (Macmillan U.S.A.)

  * Translated into other European languages, Chinese, Japanese
and Braille.

THE PRICE OF SUCCESS

An Autobiography

J. B. Phillips

D. D., Hon. D. Litt., Exeter
Canon Emeritus of Salisbury

HAROLD SHAW PUBLISHERS
WHEATON, ILLINOIS

Copyright © 1984 by J. B. Phillips

The American edition of *The Price of Success* is published by special arrangement with Hodder & Stoughton, Sevenoaks, Kent, England.

ISBN 0–87788–659–8

Cover and inside photos courtesy of Vera Phillips

Library of Congress Cataloging in Publication Data
Phillips, J. B. (John Bertram), 1906–1982
    The price of success.

    Includes index.
    1. Phillips, J. B. (John Bertram), 1906–1982
2. Church of England—Clergy—Biography.   3. Anglican
Communion—England—Clergy—Biography.   4. New Testament
scholars—England—Biography.   I. Title.
BX5199.P56A35   1984   283'.3 [B]   84–23472
ISBN 0–87788–659–8

First printing, June 1985

Contents

Foreword		7
1	Barnes	11
2	East Sheen	29
3	Adolescent struggles	44
4	Destined for the Ministry	54
5	Early Tensions	67
6	St. Margaret's, Lee, Marriage and Wartime	80
7	Letters to Young Churches	94
8	St. John's, Redhill	111
9	The First American Tour	127
10	Attitudes to the New Testament	141
11	Happiness and Success in Swanage	154
12	A Varied Ministry	170
13	Communicating	187
14	Light at the End of the Tunnel	196
Index		217

Top: Jack Phillips with his sister, Dorothy. Bottom left: Phillips (center) at Cambridge, 1925. Bottom right: J. B. Phillips marries Vera Jones, April 19, 1939, St. Margaret's, Lee.

Bombing of Church of the Good Shepherd, Lee, October, 1941, when Phillips was vicar.

The Parish Hall of the Church of the Good Shepherd restored after the bombing.

Above: Phillips autographing copies of Letters to Young Churches *in British bookshop, 1948.*

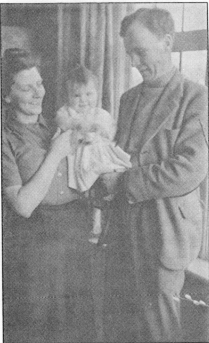

Left: Vera and Jack, with daughter, Jennifer, born in 1946.

The vicar and his wife, 1953.

Above: Phillips dictating translation to his secretary, Margery in 1956. Below: Phillips receiving th
millionth copy of Letters to Young Churches *at the London office of Macmillan Publishing Co.*

Foreword

Without Edwin Robertson this book would probably never have been published. Not long before his death Jack asked Edwin if he would complete it and, because of his love and admiration for J.B., he has been able to edit the work as I'm sure Jack would have wanted it done. They had been friends for many years and had co-operated in broadcasts as well as in the translation of *Four Prophets*, and as Jack once said "were on the same wavelength".

The writing was, of course, all J.B.'s, most of it done during his latter years when suffering from the clinical depression which was so debilitating. I played some part in the preparation of the book and I would like to thank Edwin for the very large part he played in its editing. He has been to me, as he was to Jack, "an exceptionally able, kind and quietly determined friend".

I hope the book will bring to his many worldwide friends something of "the other side" of J.B.P., my man of God. It shows, not only his beginnings and background, but some of his lifelong ambition to *communicate* and his conviction that:

"God is the great reality.

His resources are available and endless,

His promises are real and glorious beyond our wildest dreams." and:

"In Christ . . . death can be safely ignored and Heaven confidently welcomed".

Swanage, Dorset   Vera Phillips

J. B. Phillips, 1906–1982

John Bertram Phillips was born in Barnes, a suburb of London, on 16th September 1906, the second child of Philip William Phillips, O.B.E., a civil servant, and his wife, Emily Maud, who before her marriage had worked as a post office assistant. Their first child, Dorothy Maud, had been born three years before on 14th September 1903. While still living in Barnes, a third child, Kenneth Charles, was born on 16th May 1908. Their mother suffered from a long and painful illness and eventually died of cancer in 1921.

The Price of Success

I was in a state of some excitement throughout the whole of 1955. My work hardly seemed arduous for it was intrinsically exciting. I was tasting the sweets of success to an almost unimaginable degree, my health was excellent; my future prospects were rosier than my wildest dreams could ever suggest; applause, honour and appreciation met me wherever I went. I was well aware of the dangers of sudden wealth and I took some severe measures to make sure that, although comfortable, I should never be rich. I was not nearly so aware of the dangers of success. The subtle corrosion of character, the unconscious changing of values and the secret monstrous growth of a vastly inflated idea of myself seeped slowly into me. Vaguely I was aware of this and, like some frightful parody of St. Augustine, I prayed, "Lord, make me humble – but not yet". I can still savour the sweet and gorgeous taste of it all – the warm admiration, the sense of power, of overwhelming ability, of boundless energy and never failing enthusiasm. I still do not regret it; in a sense it was inevitable, for I was still very young for my age. But it is very plain to me now why my one man kingdom of power and glory had to stop.

1

Barnes

1906–1914

When I was a little child I talked and felt and thought like
a little child.

Barnes

Barnes was and is a very pleasant suburb. It is near enough
to London for easy commuting, and has hundreds of acres of
open common, park or heath land within easy reach. Barnes
has its own common and green, complete with pond; Putney
Heath is nearby and within a couple of miles or so is Richmond Park; not far away are the many acres of Wimbledon
Common.

In support of suburbia

I would like to put in a word of support for the "suburbs" or
at least the south London ones. They seem to call down the
contempt of many writers and I have honestly never been able
to see why. Most of the suburbanites I have known are good,
honest, dependable, loyal and patriotic people. They work
hard and are thrifty; they are often willing to make sacrifices
for the education or training of their children; they are law
abiding and helpful to those in trouble; they are mostly
modest and do not say very much. Most of them work for very
small salaries but they rarely complain. I suppose it is their
lack of flamboyance, their regularity of behaviour, their
limited horizons, and their general "respectability" which
irritates those of different and possibly more adventurous
character.

11

These are the people among whom I was born and brought up. In later years it was also suburban people, this time of south-east rather than south-west London, whom I was privileged to serve during the years of the blitz. I count myself lucky to have known so many of them.

Our quiet respectable suburb was peopled mainly by those with secure jobs. There were bank clerks, small businessmen, local government officials, a few railway workers of the higher grades and a few schoolteachers. I think we were a fairly typical lower middle-class group. This was my relatively peaceful and secure world and for years I knew no other.

Mother

My mother and I got on very well together. She was not the motherly type at all but both my sister (a little older than I) and my brother (a little younger) found in her a nearly perfect friend. She was highly intelligent and had a pretty wit. She never fussed over us, and rarely showed any warm affection or indeed emotion of any kind. But she was the one really dependable person around, and you could rely on her integrity. She was quick to encourage but just as prepared to cut anyone down to size if she felt it necessary.

She was in many ways a remarkable woman, and perhaps particularly so in the days of the beginning of this century, because she went out and got a job. She had no need to, for her father was quite well off by suburban standards, but she wanted to do something rather than sit at home waiting for Mr. Right to come along. Opportunities were not great but she eventually held down quite a good job in the Post Office. I think she was concerned with the Savings Bank department, but I do know that it was under the auspices, so to speak, of London's General Post Office that she met my father. She was a little older than he and it was a genuine love match. My father loved his wife deeply, as was later shown most poignantly when she was seriously ill and after a hard day's work he would do all he could to nurse and generally tend her.

Father

The only disturbing and alarming factor for me was my father. It was not only that he was big and strong and set the highest standards both for himself and everybody else, but he possessed the most enormous energy. As a rather skinny and not over-robust child I found this strength coupled with his unquenchable ambition to get on most daunting. His own father, who was someone fairly high up in the Plymouth police died suddenly, when my father was still a pupil at Plymouth grammar school.

Consequently, driven by his own desire to make something of his life, he settled in a bed-sit in London at the age of fourteen. For years he worked in one of London's postal sorting offices for a small wage, meanwhile relentlessly teaching himself accountancy as well as the elements of Latin and French. It must have taken enormous courage and determination to "scorn delights and live laborious days" – and nights – for several years. In winter, and London can be very cold, his only heating was a small oil stove. But he stuck to it and eventually embarked on an increasingly successful career, first in the ministry of health and later in the ministry of labour.

For all this I greatly admired and respected him, although he rarely mentioned his early hard work and tenacity, and certainly never boasted of it. Indeed, as time passed, he grew ashamed of the facts. He did not want any of his public school friends (of later years) to know that he had been educated at Plymouth grammar school and was thereafter largely self-educated. I should have thought it was something to be proud of, and would have been so regarded except by the ultra snobbish.

Perfectionism

I don't think I inherited this driving personal ambition, but I certainly absorbed his perfectionism and it is with me to this day. Up to a point it is good; it is surely right that a man should be severely critical of his own work and should never publish anything that falls short of his best standards. But the perfectionist obsession becomes absurd in the context of daily

13

human contact. It would be a sad thing indeed if I only had personal friendships with those of intelligence equal to, or superior to, my own. And this is happily not true. Certainly I enjoy the conversation of those with better brains than mine, but I have friends, much valued friends, in various walks of life.

The only way in which perfectionism is a nuisance is that it prevents me from enjoying anything in the world of arts unless it is really well done. This makes it hard to be polite, let alone truthful, if I am asked to comment on a poor amateur dramatic performance, a bad painting, an indifferent ballet or an earnest but excruciating musical performance.

Mental dexterity

Luckily for me I had a pretty bright mind and a memory that was nearly photographic. Thus in my earliest schooldays it was not hard to be top of the form or at least in the first three. I simply could not understand how people could get things *wrong*. If you didn't know a fact, well, fair enough, you didn't know it and you lost a mark. But if you had been taught a fact, I could not see how you could then forget it. This accuracy led me from time to time into trouble with other little boys (and girls). I used to try and avoid getting ten out of ten by making deliberate mistakes, or by leaving blank a question the answer to which I knew perfectly well. And this didn't really help much, for I was, and am, an obsessive teller of the truth. I literally could not lie and if faced with a direct question from a perceptive teacher I was bound to confess that I really *did* know. But apart from occasional bouts of unpopularity, and the disadvantage of not being physically very strong, I enjoyed my various schools almost all the time.

All this precocious mental dexterity plainly delighted my father, but my mother was always ready with a kind but withering remark in case I became what St. Paul called "puffed up". Not that I would have it thought that I was mentally advanced in all directions. For example, although I was very fond of music and could pick out a melody on the piano by ear with one finger, I was musically *dyslexic*. I simply could not understand musical notation; I could not see why, if

14

I was required to play a note of A, they shouldn't say so in print (and similarly mark the key on the piano, as they did on typewriters) instead of using these cumbersome staves of treble and bass and all the curious signs marked on or between the five lines of each stave. Further, it bothered me that musical notation (for both hands for Heaven's sake) was marked *vertically*, while the piano keyboard was horizontal.

I just could not make sense of this, although my sister played quite well and retained the gift of instant harmonisation into later life. My brother, too, although he gave it up fairly soon, could play the piano in simple fashion.

So, although after hearing a new descant to a hymn at a church service, I could come home and reproduce it (with one finger) on the piano with accuracy, I could not read a note of printed music, however simple. Nobody really blamed me for this, although it was considered a little odd, but I used to feel a complete idiot at this inability, and concentrated all the more on words and, in those days, figures.

Musical and other sensitivities

My other musical bother was that I could really only hear one part at a time. It was years later that I came to appreciate even a trio, and even later to take in the complex sound of a full orchestra. At Christmas-time when many carols were sung, with or without friends and relations, my sister would dart about from soprano to the alto or even to the tenor part sung an octave higher; others joined in according to their musical ability (everybody in those days seemed to be able to sing) while I was always stuck with the melody only.

Sometimes when alone in the room I would strike a single note, usually down in the bass, with the loud pedal down and my ear close to the wooden case of the piano. This single note was full of fairy magic to me and its reverberations, even though of only a few seconds duration, conjured up for me unfathomable mysteries. I think, at the age of six or seven, I was considered a little eccentric, and it wasn't until many years later that I received some consolation from no less a person than Malcolm Arnold. I told him of my early experiences – how strongly music moved me, even though I could

15

only absorb one note at a time. He replied to the effect that I must really be genuinely musical, and this cheered me a lot.

I have suffered all my life from an extreme vulnerability to sights and sounds which apparently left others slightly, if at all, moved. All colours were too bright for me, all sounds too loud or too complex, and almost every taste and smell was much too violent for my tongue or nose. The strong sunlight of summer holidays by the sea was far too much for my sight and every sunny day meant painfully screwed-up eyes as well as a skin only too ready to burn painfully (but never to tan). No one ever thought that a child might need dark glasses in those days, but I grew to hate the really sunny days.

With this intense physical sensory perception of light, colour, sound, taste and smell went a general nervous sensitivity. I could feel atmosphere sharply and detect friendliness or hostility even if no word was spoken. I think my father, although himself a healthy extrovert and not very sensitive, did try to make allowances for me, his bright and promising son. But I don't think he ever understood my very real fear of cold sea water nor my apprehensive dread at having to meet new people or face new experiences. He was certainly disappointed that I was thin, had little appetite and was far from muscular.

In face of my father's vigour and perfectionist demands we three children reacted in different ways. My sister always strove to please, though in her childhood she had never learned pretty ways or feminine wiles. My brother pretended to be much more stupid than he really was. This was a wise move really, since before long my father left him alone. For myself, the only way out of an intolerable situation seemed to me to get so high above my father that he could not reach me. Since this was impossible physically I tried with all my mind, photographic memory and all, to reach an unreachable pinnacle. To some extent this worked, but unhappily the neurotic drive behind it continued, with occasional abatements, for many years after it ceased to be useful. Much unnecessary strain would have been avoided if I had discarded this super-perfectionism years before I did.

Belief in God

I think I must have been born a believer in God, as very early remembered experience seems to show. This does not mean that I was born a Christian with an *anima naturaliter Christiana* – quite the contrary. I certainly had my share of original sin and to this day I envy people who can, apparently without effort, be unselfish, kind, generous and good. I only achieve these things by continual self-discipline and prayer, by deliberate thought and the exercise of will. I know myself only too well to disbelieve in original sin.

I could not have been more than three-and-a-half years old when, on a cold starlit night, I became aware of the immensity of the Creation that I could see. By easy inference the Creator Himself must be infinitely vaster. I felt very small and very awed. I can remember reflecting, "If he stops thinking about me I shall not exist at all." A sobering thought for a very small boy and nearer to the truth than he guessed.

But this sense of God, which has appeared and disappeared throughout my life, had little to do with my father's religious instruction, or that which I later heard at school. My father was a tall, strong and in those days very irritable and impatient man, driven by ambition and often ridden with anxiety. He frightened me very deeply, not that I think he ever, except in a very minor way, assaulted me physically. But he was a perfectionist, and what is more, a God-fearing, church-going perfectionist. To me he personified some of the least attractive features of the Old Testament Jehovah. If you were good and produced first-class results he loved you, but if you didn't, well, "woe unto you and woe!" I can remember his saying to me once, "Now you know I love you; remember that God loves you infinitely more." This artless saying filled me with indescribable terror.

Not long before he died I used to talk to my father about this fear-ridden period, and he could not understand, or indeed believe in it. But if you have a strong, ambitious and righteous father on the one hand and a rather under-sized imaginative, intelligent and sensitive small boy on the other it pays to be a watchful as well as a loving parent. It took me years to get over this father image, what William Blake called, I think, the

17

Nobodaddy, and for quite a time it cast a dark shadow over my thoughts of God.

Early education

I could tell the time before I was four years old, and taught myself to read soon afterwards. I did this by studying illustrated books of *the Cat-Sat-On-The-Mat* variety and by reading nursery rhymes with pictures. Before many months I was reading everything I could lay hands on. It didn't really matter if I came across unfamiliar words, for the context sooner or later made their meaning plain. The only trouble was that I was usually too proud, or conceited, to ask how words were pronounced. Normal conversation answered most of the questions and I was lucky in being brought up in an intelligent home.

I was further fortunate in being sent at a very early age to the local dame school where reasonable conversation was as important as learning the elements of arithmetic or English history. Nevertheless it was years before I realised that the boy's Christian name Denys was pronounced Dennis and not Denies. Even today, although I am a quick reader, I am in fact pronouncing words as I go along (No, I don't move my lips!). Thus even in my fastest reading I can detect good, rhythmical balance as well as unpleasant dissonances.

Boat race

I started life in a terraced house, but houses were well built, roads were broad and kept clean while everybody had a small but neat and well-kept garden. Nearby flowed the river Thames and every year I was taken to see the annual Oxford and Cambridge boat race. I can remember when I was very young indeed being held up in someone's arms while I waved a paper streamer for Oxford. (Who chose *Oxford* for me I don't remember.) The enthusiasm shown on both banks of the river for almost the entire course was alarming to me then (because noisy crowds were frightening), and astonishes me today. The event is not really of world-shaking importance, but the television cameras still show pretty large crowds lining the tow path, often in a biting wind with rain and sometimes snow to add to the general discomfort. The same keen parti-sanship for either the light-blue or the dark-blue oars moving so swiftly and beautifully apparently is an enduring part of the British (or at least London) tradition.

Childhood

Apart from the stresses and anxieties I have hinted at above, my childhood was certainly as happy as any other sensitive child's. We were, it seemed to me, very poor and, although this never reached the stage of going hungry, there were no extras in the way of presents, and no treats except at Christmas-time. My father always impressed upon us the need for the utmost economy. None of us was extravagant by nature I think, and the caution was hardly necessary. But it was depressing to find that my weekly penny of pocket money was expected to go, by means of a red penny stamp stuck on a paper slip, straight into the post office savings bank.

It was painful, and sometimes embarrassing in the presence of other children, to have no money to buy sweets. These were bought for us, by the jar, from the civil service stores, and doled out to us a very few at a time. This was regarded as an economy as well as a safeguard against our buying un-wholesome or dangerous sweets at the many tempting little sweet shops. (The situation would have been far worse if there had been ice-cream for sale, but in our world, except rarely at a party, there was none.)

Father's anxieties

I admit that my father was not earning much of an income and that he was buying, on mortgage, the house in which we were living. But his agitation and anxiety over the smallest extra expense seemed to me exaggerated to the point of absurdity. If a slate blew off the roof, for example, we were immediately told of ruin and disaster. For my father to have even a small overdraft at the bank was equivalent to a public declaration of bankruptcy. Bills were always paid at once, as if we would all go to prison if they were not. "We can't afford it" was a frequently heard expression in our little house.

19

Nevertheless I could not help noticing that my father did not hesitate to buy, for himself, a small greenhouse, an expensive-looking mandoline and later a good clarinet. I didn't grudge him these things but I think life would have been easier if my mother hadn't had to manage housekeeping on such a tight budget, and if we, the three children, had occasionally a few coppers in our purses or pockets. I cannot believe that a slight relaxation in economy would have led to the Unspeakable Overdraft.

I recall vividly one little incident which must have happened when I was about five years old. It made me laugh (very secretly) at the time, but it was treated by my father as a national disaster. What happened was this. My father, possibly through his incessant pipe-smoking, had a sore throat. To ease this he bought some potassium chlorate tablets – quite a common relieving agent in those days. Unhappily the bottle (or cardboard pill-box) spilled its contents into my father's side-pocket. They came in contact with some rubber bands which were already nestling there. The friction produced in the side-pocket of the jacket of an active man is no doubt considerable, and there was a sudden and alarming conflagration in the office. No one was hurt and no damage was done except to the jacket, but when my father arrived home we all heard the story as though from an eye-witness of the Great Fire of London.

Once more ruin and disaster stared us in the face. My father, coatless, jobless and probably homeless was plunged into a vision of utter failure.

My mother maintained her usual commonsense attitude and finally persuaded my father that he had another jacket and that the damaged one could be repaired. (It was, too, quite quickly and at the cost of a very few shillings.) But my father took some time to recover from this dastardly blow of fate. He did not brood but plunged into his clerical work, his house-decorating or his gardening with even more frantic energy than before.

I may say, in passing, that he really was an excellent gardener, knowing instinctively, it seemed, what to do and when to do it. Even this little garden in Barnes seemed to bloom perpetually and to produce excellent vegetables. And, many years later, my father tamed several windswept barren acres of the North Downs in Surrey, working (except in darkest winter) after office hours with only occasional help from a jobbing gardener. He made a splendid job of it.

I don't know whether it was because I was early dragooned into "helping" or whether I had an innate distaste for the back-breaking, time-consuming and generally dirty work of making and maintaining a garden, but I hate gardening. The everlasting spraying, dusting, pruning, thinning out, forking over and tying back fill me with a kind of bored dismay. Of course I love *gardens*; who doesn't. But the actual work of gardening has no appeal for me, and what I do I do more for the sake of appearances than for anything else.

Barnes before the First World War

We lived in Barnes for over eight years and, apart from childish fears and occasional terrifying nightmares, they were happy years for me. There was no motor traffic on our roads. What little traffic there was was drawn by horses, and apart from tradesmen, "dustmen" (as we then called them) and an occasional visit in summer by a water-spraying vehicle – to "lay the dust" as they said – there was virtually no threat from traffic. We could, and did, play in the streets without any danger. Milk was delivered daily by means of what looked like an outsize dairy churn, covered in summer with a canvas coat. It was dispensed into milk cans, which were apparently made of some pewter-like material with a brass label on the top engraved with the capacity of the particular vessel. These we were expected to, and did, keep spotlessly clean our-selves. When I read today that a *million and a half* milk bottles are lost, broken or stolen every day I cannot feel that we have progressed.

Butcher's meat and groceries were always delivered by a young man on a bicycle fitted with a capacious metal carrying basket over his front wheel. Coal was delivered by the horse-drawn coal cart. It was always in hundredweight bags and the prudent housewife was expected to count these as they were poured into her coal store or cellar. In later years I tried to lift a similar bag of 112 pounds and it was as much as I could manage. But to those grimy-faced and usually cheerful coal-men the work seemed to cause little trouble.

I do not remember the slightest snobbery or sense of keeping up with the Joneses. I think this was partly because we who lived in Barnes were all more or less of the same social grade, and there were no marked differences in dress and outward possessions. It is true that some had slightly larger houses, some gave more lavish parties for children and some girls had more, and gayer, dresses than my own sister. But I honestly do not remember encountering any envy or malice expressed about or towards the slightly better off.

Uncle Charles

No one owned a horse-drawn vehicle (except the two local doctors) and certainly only one man owned a car. This was the possession of my Uncle Charles, my mother's brother, who lived a few hundred yards away. He was certainly not re-garded with envy but looked upon as mildly eccentric. His car was, I think, a single-cylindered Swift but to my knowledge it very rarely emerged on the public roads. As children we used to sit on its splendidly upholstered leather seats as it sat in its wooden garage. We used to make the sort of "poop, poop" noises made, as we learnt years later, by the immortal Mr. Toad of *The Wind in the Willows*.

Uncle Charles' other eccentricity was that his house, the only house in the district to be so equipped, was lighted by electricity. This was the more remarkable since he occupied quite a good position in the powerful Gas, Light and Coke Company. I never understood this, and I believed for years that employees of any gas-supplying firm were in honour bound to use only gas for their lighting and heating. Certainly all the rest of us cooked by gas and illuminated our best rooms with incandescent "mantles" and the smaller domestic offices with "fish-tail" burners. I don't suppose these fish-tail flames at their most blazing used any less gas than the more respect-able and light-giving mantles. But they had the advantage that they could be turned down to a mere glimmer, and economy was in our hearts a lot of the time. In any case Uncle

Charles was an eccentric and if he chose to own a car and light his house by expensive electricity as well, good luck to him.

Class

The only form of class consciousness that came my way in these early days was caused by the occasional appearances of gangs of dirty and ill-clad boys who came, we supposed, from the lower haunts of Mortlake, a neighbouring suburb. They never, as far as I can remember, appeared singly but always in gangs of a dozen or twenty, armed with catapults, sticks and stones. Their age would range from about eight to fourteen, and as my eyes saw them as groups of ruffians I kept out of their way. They were the vandals of the day and would destroy window-panes of empty houses, break the glass of street lamps, overturn and break if possible the benches on Barnes Common, deface posters, pull down shaky fences and in fact do all the other acts of senseless destruction in which their grandsons and great grandsons indulge today.

Only once did I see two or three of these louts caught and it made a deep impression on me. They had started a gorse fire – a very easy thing to do, for in those days Barnes Common was dotted with clumps of gorse and broom. Two Common-keepers, formidably uniformed in brown bowler hats, brown Norfolk jackets and breeches, and brown leather leggings and boots, had caught these young arsonists running away from what soon became a considerable blaze. A fair crowd collected, the horse-drawn fire-engine thundered up within minutes and the blaze was quickly brought under control. The wretched boys, pale-faced and shivering with fright by now, were in the grip of the stalwart keepers. One of them piped up in a scared voice, "Can we go now, sir, now the fire's out?" "Not on your life, son," replied the senior keeper. "It'll be prison for all of you, you see!" I don't suppose that it did mean a prison sentence but at the time I felt the power of the Law (though the keepers were not, in fact, policemen) and even a slight pang of pity for the wretched little rogues who had put themselves in such peril.

Religious practice

Most of us suburbanites were pretty regular church-goers, and for us this meant morning service in Barnes parish church and, later on, morning *and* evening services. I didn't resent this at the time; it was all part of the pattern of life. But neither do I remember any part of the service which appealed to me, except perhaps for some of the hymns. Certainly the "religious sense" to which I referred earlier was never stimulated by a Church of England mattins or evensong.

For a time we had family prayers immediately after breakfast at home. The form was adapted from the Anglican *Book of Common Prayer*, and seemed to me the epitome of vain repetitions. No one could say that my father was a good reader and since the exercise was often taken at a hurried pace I was relieved when it quietly faded from the scene. The reason for this discontinuance was never disclosed.

My religious life at this time hardly existed as a reality with any relevance to life. It is true that I said my prayers every evening; it would have felt as wrong had I not done so as if I had omitted to brush my teeth or wash my face, neck and hands. I knew the Ten Commandments by heart by the time I was five years old, but they rang no answering bells in my heart. I had no desire to carve a graven image, still less to worship it. Murder was understandably forbidden, and adultery was meaningless and never explained. I was never tempted to steal but I agreed that it was wrong. I wasn't much disposed to covet at all, and certainly not my neighbour's ox or his ass, since he had neither. As a guide to life the Ten Commandments seemed to me totally valueless.

My father was not a strict Sabbatarian, though he believed in the day of rest and tried to avoid causing unnecessary work for others as much as he could. Apart from the compulsory going to church we did not find Sunday particularly burdensome. I think I was probably about eight years old when my father thought we ought to learn the Collect for the Day. Later, perhaps at the age of ten, we were put through the catechism contained in the *Book of Common Prayer*. This again, though only fairly intelligible, was easy enough, and I quickly found myself able to give the prescribed answers to the

24

prescribed questions. There was a certain rhythm to the old-fashioned language which pleased my ear, and I can remember being particularly pleased by the definition of a sacrament. "An outward and visible sign of an inward and spiritual grace" struck me then as a lucid and felicitous definition, and it still does. I also used to wonder a bit about the "pomps and vanity of this wicked world", which my godparents had apparently renounced in my name at my baptism. Indeed I rather wondered if I should recognise a pomp or a vanity if I saw one, but I can't say it bothered me much.

Wandsworth

My mother's parents lived in Allfarthing Lane, Wandsworth. We used to go there sometimes at weekends, by horse-bus. The horses were always changed at the foot of East Hill. To me this was always a rather alarming move. Indeed sometimes I wondered if the driver had somehow failed; it did not strike me for years that it was for the sake of the *horses* that the change was made, and had nothing to do with the competence or incompetence of the drivers.

The house at Allfarthing Lane struck me as large and imposing. My grandfather was a private secretary (whatever that was) and with him lived, in comparative affluence, my grandmother and two maiden aunts. The house was splendidly furnished in the late Victorian style, and it had a *cellar*. This seemed a wonderful dark cave of mystery to me, smelling sharply of coal and storing some bottles of wines and spirits. My grandfather was not a teetotaller like my father, and enjoyed his food. Moreover he had a billiards table – an almost unheard of luxury in our circle. I don't suppose it was a very large one, but I well remember its presence when I was sent to kiss grandpa good night. I also remember the prickliness of his beard, and the not unpleasant smell of cigar and brandy on his breath.

I don't remember how often we went to the Wandsworth home, but I can remember spending at least one Christmas there. The food and drink were splendid, and although as children we were not allowed wine we were given lemonade out of a *blue* sodawater syphon. To me it tasted like nectar.

If we were at Wandsworth on Sundays we went to St. Anne's church. I was baptised there, and one of the curates, a close friend of my father, was destined to become principal of Westcott House, Cambridge. My chief memories of that church were its "pepper-pot" steeple, which I hope is still there, and its clamorous bells.

Now bells across the meadow are one thing, but bells beating into your brain and even, seemingly, vibrating your whole body are another. To me, even today, bells except at a proper distance are a musical torture. Not one of them seems to me to have a musically true note but is invariably hag-ridden with harmonics and overtones. As I sat in the pew at St. Anne's, Wandsworth, what beat at my poor ears was not so much the fundamental peals but the excruciating inter-action of the assorted harmonics of the whole body of bells.

Somewhere along these early years of weekly church-going I grew very critical of words, both in the liturgy and especially of hymns. I could appreciate the poetry of such lines as "risen with healing in his wings", or "all wreaths of empire meet upon his brow" even though they were not making any real prose *sense*. Many hymns tickled my all too easily aroused sense of humour. I will mention one, since it has haunted me for years. In one of the verses we sang to the Almighty, "Lord, give me Samuel's ear". I didn't want Samuel's ear, and wouldn't know what to do with it if I had it. But the hymn writer not only asks for an ear, but specifies *which* one he wants, i.e. "the open one, O Lord". This was, and is, too much for me.

School

I used to walk to my dame school (it was about three-quarters of a mile) and I never really thought about the weather. One or two things stand out in my memory. One was the occasion (so rare that I think it was unique) when the young assistant was so completely exasperated by our obtuse-ness that she lost her temper and shouted, "You're hopeless! you might as well go home!" and then flounced out of the room. We all, a small class of about a dozen, took this to mean that we were being told to go home. So down we trooped to a sort of conservatory room where outdoor boots (rarely, if ever, shoes) overcoats and hats were hung or put on racks. Slowly and rather fearfully we began to change into our outdoor clothes. But within a few minutes the head girl, a large and menacing girl of possibly eleven years of age, appeared, and said in a voice shaking with fury, "You little gooses, what do you think you're doing? Get on back to your form room!" This we did, and the lesson was resumed without further comment. For myself I made a mental note that if big girls were sufficiently agitated they could forget their knowledge of the English language.

Since I could read and to some degree write, I was, with several others, put to the task of copy-book writing. For this you copied a maxim or proverb printed in immaculate "copper-plate" in a cursive script with thin up-strokes and thick down-strokes. You did this three times on "feint" lines beneath each printed precept, and it was expected that your third attempt should be the best. I don't think this exercise did us any harm at all, indeed it helped us to concentrate and probably improved co-ordination between hand and eye. But I was puzzled, though not worried, by the *sense* of what I copied. What on earth could "A stitch in time saves nine" or "Procrastination is the thief of time" possibly mean? I don't honestly think this exercise, quite enjoyable as it was, had much influence on my actual handwriting. But at least the use of pen and ink for "copper-plate" writing did show clearly why some lines are thin and some thick. The tradition was passed on into the art of printing and remains with few exceptions, in all modern print and lettering. Capital letters like A, W, M or N, for example, look very odd indeed if the thicks and thins are transposed.

I think this particular dame school in Barnes must have been an exceptionally good one. I was very well taught and fairly treated and had many friends of both sexes. At any rate by the time I left I had what used to be called a very good grounding in English, both in grammar and syntax, an excellent if limited knowledge of the uses of arithmetic and an ability to put down thoughts in words. Of course we were also taught such things as history and geography, but they consisted almost entirely of learning lists of kings and queens or of the capes, rivers and lakes, of my own country.

2

East Sheen
1914–1921

What do you want most out of life? Well, perhaps it's success, everyone looking up to you etc. No more feelings of
inferiority, you're at the top of the tree. Well, success is all
right if you've done good work and kept the rules. But the
happy successful people have found success was a by-
product. They were aiming at something else, such as
being really good at the things they were best suited for,
and success came as a kind of bonus. The people who aim
at success very rarely get it. And some of them, behind the
"success" are pretty miserable.

The First World War

I remember quite well my sister reading the news of the
outbreak of war to my brother and myself, and our frank
disbelief. In our limited sheltered life war just did not happen – could not be imagined at all. But the war did come;
patriotic posters, detestation of all that was German, the
heart-warming sense that we, *Great* Britain, were going to the
rescue of poor little Belgium – all these things affected my
eight-year-old mind and, like almost everyone else, I became
intensely patriotic. We were not much affected by the first two
years of that war. True, some of the young men we knew were
called up but neither my father nor any uncles were affected.
They must have been in their late thirties and were probably
"deferred". But I think they all joined some military service,
either as special constables or as the equivalent of what is
known today as "Dad's Army".

It was in the summer of 1914 that we moved to East Sheen

Avenue, which in those days really was an avenue lined with magnificent elm trees (felled, alas, some years ago). I am still puzzled that at the beginning of a war private building was still going on. But it certainly was, and we moved from a terraced house into a three-storey semi-detached, while the "other half" was still being built. It seemed a big step-up in the world to me. I can remember quite vividly an oak-panelled hall (instead of a hall passage) and can still smell the glue which was used for the genuine parquet floor. Of course the house and garden were not really big at all but they seemed big to me then. And instead of the gorse-studded Barnes Common the real country, complete with buttercups and daisies, with birds and rabbits, was less than a hundred yards away. Beyond these lovely green fields (lovely, that is, apart from a patch of "allotments" which my father and others worked at unceasingly) there was Beverley Brook – where I saw my first kingfisher – and then, through the Roehampton Gate, the apparently boundless acres of Richmond Park.

Soon we first began to feel the pinch of war. We became accustomed to "marge" instead of butter, and to use Cook's Farmhouse Eggs (dried) instead of the usual new laid. Rationing must have been in force, but never having been a big eater, I can't say I noticed it much. My father produced a lot of vegetables from the allotment and that must have helped a good deal. Fruit appeared very rarely, except during the season of the English apple crop. Air raids were very few in the daylight, but towards the end of the war raids at night were fairly frequent and even the dreaded Zeppelins occasionally appeared. Considering the extreme vulnerability of these huge affairs, filled with highly inflammable hydrogen gas, I was and still am, astonished that they were not immediately shot down. Several times I saw one pinned in the beams of our searchlights, but only once did I see one hit, burst into flames and crash some miles away. I recollect being told to "remember" it; I am not sure why. Perhaps it was to remind me that the anti-aircraft gunners, who made a tremendous noise with their so-called barrage did in fact sometimes hit something.

Alice

In 1915, soon after moving into the new house, we acquired a living-in maid, by name of Alice. She was a treasure in every way. We did not know it then, but in fact my mother was already suffering considerable pain from cancer. We simply noticed that mother always seemed tired, and were honestly grateful that Alice was able to do most of the housework and cooking. I think my mother used to retire to bed early, for I can remember quite clearly many times having supper with Alice in the kitchen. This was a cosy room, especially in the winter since one wall of it was entirely occupied by a coal-burning stove-cum-boiler, with an oven and numerous hotplates. These monstrous affairs were commonplace in our class of society. I think they were called "kitcheners", and I used to wonder vaguely if they were invented by the military figure who, with piercing eyes and spiked moustache, stared at us from every hoarding.

It was in 1916, or possibly 1917, that we had three soldiers billeted on us. All three were amusing and well mannered guests. All three, after a few weeks' training in the nearby camp in Richmond Park, were sent to France. In a matter of months all three were killed in one of the bloody battles across the Channel, where already millions of lives had been lost. I think as children we accepted this as one of the inevitabilities of war, but we were none the less sad to lose such interesting and amusing friends.

Schools

Educationally I did not fare very well at this time. For a few brief months I was sent to another dame school, which was about as bad as the other one was good. This one was overcrowded, ill-disciplined and noisy, and I don't remember learning anything at all.

After that I was sent to an establishment purporting to be a "preparatory school for the sons of gentlemen". My father must have been taken in by the advertisement, for it was academically beneath even my ten-year-old needs. It was run by a peculiarly nasty little Welshman, with one ill paid assistant. (How did I know he was ill paid? Well, no one who had frayed cuffs, collars and trouser bottoms, and who apparently used one and the same handkerchief for a whole term could have been paid a proper salary.) The little Welshman was not only ignorant but a sadist. He is the only man I have ever met who positively drooled over causing pain to others. Anything, or nothing, would bring one within the range of his cane, and we all suffered in some degree. The thing I remember chiefly was not so much the pain as the gross injustice. This man would punish, not for some offence such as inattention or failure to do homework, but for simply not knowing the answer to some foolish question which he had just thought up. I did not stay at that so-called college for long.

Extra-curricular activities

Fortunately for me I found the *Children's Encyclopedia* a most useful supplementary source of information, and although I don't remember the original set of volumes ever being replaced I used them repeatedly from the age of nine until I was twelve or so. The basic principles of such diverse subjects as cotton spinning, newspaper printing, early aviation, cloud formation, the colours of the spectrum, the formation of the planetary system and a score of other subjects were pounced upon by my ever-inquisitive mind. The chief gaps were that I could find nothing about the internal combustion engine, although motor cars were becoming a fairly common sight by the beginning of the First World War and the horse-drawn buses were being replaced by the petrol-driven solid tyred, open scarlet monsters of the London General Omnibus Company.

Neither did I find anything useful about the uses of electricity, whether to produce light, heat or power to drive such things as trams, which ran on rails on main roads only a few miles away.

The other "educational" agent to me was the possession of that mechanical do-it-yourself constructional kit called Meccano. Unfortunately I was restricted to the more elementary sets, and had to be content with strings and pulleys when I longed for gear-wheels and pinions. Nevertheless, such manual dexterity as I have developed in later years probably owes much to countless models which I constructed from those nickel-plated girders with brass nuts and bolts.

The entrance examination

My father had decided that, since he could not afford public school fees, I should go to a London day school, whose organisation was based on public school lines. Thus I soon found myself sitting for the entrance examination for Emanuel School, Wandsworth Common – not many miles away. (This school was founded in 1594 by Lady Dacre in Westminster, and has a long and honourable history.) I well remember that both my father and mother accompanied me. We went by electric train from Mortlake to Clapham Junction and then walked to the school. (A journey I was to repeat hundreds of times for over seven years.) I remember the enormous length of the school drive (it *is* very long), but more sharply the length of the examination itself. It seemed to me to be by no means very difficult but it did *go on*. Eventually I grew tired and cut the last paper (which I think was French translation) and walked out. I had no watch and felt very forlorn and bewildered. I can even remember morbid thoughts of the whole operation being designed to get rid of me (I think I must have been unusually tiresome during the preceding weeks and felt that perhaps even my mother had had enough of me.) At any rate, just before I was reduced to tears, they both turned up. Nothing much was said, but I certainly did not volunteer the information that I had cut the programme short. The consequence of this *bêtise* on my part was that when I duly entered the school I was put into Form 2b, a fairly low grade. Within a few weeks I was promoted to 3a – a move not popular with either my fellows or the teaching staff.

Holidays

I think the visits to my grandparents in Wandsworth fell off soon after we moved to East Sheen, partly, I now imagine, because of my mother's failing health. Later on, the Wandsworth family moved to Branksome, near Bournemouth. My grandfather had retired but died shortly afterwards. We now found visits to Bournemouth were only for holidays.

The thought of holidays reminds me that my father, despite his constant anxieties about money and general close-fistedness, was invariably generous about holidays. Indeed for two or three weeks a year he became a different, much younger and carefree man. Several times we went to the Isle of Wight, chiefly to Shanklin, of which I retain the happiest memories, despite the bright light and inevitable sunburning. Once, in 1919, I think, when my mother had become a very sick woman, we ventured as far as Salcombe in south Devon. It was altogether delightful to finish the long train journey from London to Kingsbridge by proceeding down the estuary aboard a small steamboat.

My father also saw to it that we had a good Christmas. All sorts of goodies (muscatels and almonds, crystallised fruits, ginger in jars, tangerines and nuts of all kinds) appeared at Christmas-time, but not at any other time of the year. We went in for decorations in a big way, and for weeks beforehand we, the three children, were busy pasting together paper chains and working little artistic trifles with green leaves and tinsel. None of us, I think, ever believed in Santa Claus or Father Christmas, but we were quite prepared to go along with the current myth and duly hung up our stockings on Christmas Eve.

After 1915 and we had settled down into the new house, my father really went to town over Christmas decorations. He would paint on canvas an enormous snow scene and this would occupy the whole of one side of the oak-panelled hall. Around this effort the lesser decorations could be tastefully arranged, and the general effect was magical. The strange thing about my father's artistic activity is that he could *copy* with quite extraordinary fidelity almost any painting or colour print. Letters written to his wife during their courting days, were contained in envelopes beautifully decorated with drawings of animals and houses.

Christ Church, East Sheen

Soon after our arrival at East Sheen we changed our church allegiance to the local Christ Church, itself, I believe, a daughter church of the mother parish church of Mortlake. The church was always well filled. In the background there was some argument going on about some high church innovations proposed by the vicar. I never understood what this was all about, and I doubt if it would interest me much today. I do, however, remember the erecting of a wrought-iron screen between choir and chancel. I thought it hideous and its only effect was to render the choir slightly less audible.

I am ashamed to say that my most lasting memories of Christ Church, East Sheen, were (a) some bad sermons preached by newly ordained curates, which invariably made me, mentally not physically, grind my teeth and reflect, "If I couldn't do better than that I wouldn't ever be a clergyman." And (b) my years long silent worship of a golden-haired girl who came most regularly to church with, I presumed, her grandmother. In all the years of adoration we never exchanged a single word nor did she even once smile at me. But, strangely, her appearance is still photographically clear.

Serious illness

It must have been just before I actually started at Emanuel School that I had my first experience of nearly dying. I had somehow contracted a poisoned finger, which nobody paid much attention to. However, the infection spread rapidly to my lungs (a phenomenon which is still inexplicable to me) and I was pretty quickly a helpless patient with murmurs of "double pneumonia" and "pleurisy" sounding faintly in my ears. I didn't really feel ill but breathing was a bit painful and I was overwhelmed by a deep lethargy. I could not eat and only drank such things as barley water.

It was obvious to me that everyone from the doctor downwards thought I was not long for this world. My father became extremely gentle and my mother sat by my bed for many hours. One night in particular I felt that my earthly race was run, and in a sense I quite looked forward to the next life.

I have never been afraid of death; of pain, yes, and of mutilation, but never of the death of the body. My only regret at what I thought was my imminent decease was the pain and anxiety which could be plainly read on my mother's face. I tried to reassure her but I was too weak to form the words. I

35

fell asleep, honestly believing that I should wake in a better world.

But sometime in the small hours I suddenly felt I had turned a corner. Frankly I was disappointed, for although on the whole I enjoyed life it was always a struggle to me. It would have been only too easy to "lay down my arms". However, I was evidently meant to battle on, and on the doctor's visit on the following morning he said, "I think we can safely say he is out of danger."

Thereafter followed some tiresome weeks of convalescence – tiresome because I was too weak to read for any length of time and such toys as can be enjoyed in bed bored me almost to tears. However, it was not long before I was ordered to "run wild for about six weeks". This seemed a most enchanting prospect to me, but in fact it meant that my mother took me to Branksome, to stay with her mother and sisters. Here I recovered strength, but there wasn't much "running wild"; everyone was far too anxious that I should not "do too much", or, worse still, catch a chill and develop pneumonia for a second time. Nevertheless I roamed the then unbuilt-over woods of Branksome, the wild dunes of Canford Cliffs and explored the sandstone slopes of Branksome Chine.

A school in wartime

Soon after this, just before my eleventh birthday, I began at Emanuel School. We all know what tricks the memory plays, but I honestly believe that I enjoyed the next seven years of school greatly. I made many friends and never found the work too difficult.

The great disadvantage was nobody's fault; it was the natural consequence of the First World War. There were no young men on the staff at all, and we were taught by old men called back from retirement or, later on, by young *women* just out of training college. It was inevitable that we were inadequately taught. This did not really matter very much up to School Certificate standard (roughly the equivalent of today's O levels). I had a thirst for knowledge and could readily learn from books. Arithmetic, algebra, geometry, English, French and chemistry were easily passed by most of us. But, to our dismay, we all scored low marks in English. Later we discovered that the aged master who taught us had not read the instructions properly and had totally failed to teach us the set book, which was (Heaven help us) Carlyle's turgid and boring book, *Sartor Resartus*. This meant that some thirty or forty of us had to take (as external students) what was popularly known as the London Matric in the following term. This examination was held on a gloomy November day in, of all places, the Science Museum in South Kensington. There we sat with ancient flying machines suspended over our heads and our sides flanked by ancient locomotives. I think we all passed successfully.

Mother's death

But I have leapt ahead some three years. At home life went on in rather a minor key as my mother became increasingly ill. She rarely complained and then only of tiredness, but I now know that she suffered from cancer in various parts of her body for some ten years. She finally died in hospital in 1921 (when my father could no longer nurse her). I used to sit with her sometimes in the summer of that year, and she had become a terrible sight. She had lost almost all her hair, her body had shrunken to a tortured lump of flesh, and the pain was very great.

Most of the time in those last months she hardly knew us, and I grew angrier and angrier that God could allow such terrifying physical and mental degradation to happen to such a wonderful woman. I gave up my religious faith utterly, for what use was prayer and talk of the love of God when I returned daily to this horrible caricature of the spritely, witty mother I had known and loved? I became, as I thought, a confirmed atheist. The problem of human suffering is, I believe, the biggest serious obstacle to faith in a God of love today.

School life

However, when one is young and very busy one does not brood. Emanuel School provided all the stimulus, activity and society that I needed. The school was run on public-school lines. We had houses, house prefects and a head prefect. Discipline was strict but never unreasonable. Corporal punishment could be administered by house prefects for the more serious offences. I do not remember that this practice was abused, or resented. It was accepted as a normal part of school life.

I don't recollect any serious bullying at any time, although naturally a good deal of good-humoured ragging went on. I don't remember any snobbery either, except that we occasionally would remark sarcastically that so-and-so was "only a scholarship boy". This meant that the boy in question had won a free place at Emanuel from the elementary schools of Wandsworth or Clapham. The jibe was never continued, and the disparaging remark was made without malice; it was far more intended to prevent a new boy from getting too big for his boots than to put him outside any imaginary "pale".

I think I was twelve years old when I won two scholarships in one week, one to a free place at my present school plus a bonus of fifteen pounds a year, and the other to a free place at a boarding school called Sutton Valence (which was ruled by the same Board of Governors as Emanuel). Probably through reading too much fiction, I had developed a terror of boarding schools. They seemed to me places of terrible brutality and desperate loneliness, and I begged to stay on where I was. Not without some reservations my father consented to this, and shortly afterwards presented me with a bicycle – from, of course, the civil service stores.

I was admittedly a bright boy, but only a matter of a few months or a year were to pass before I realised that I was by no means a natural scholar. I was, and am, deeply interested in a score of widely diverse subjects but it took me a long time to learn the concentration and self-discipline which real scholarship demands.

Air raids

From 1916 until the armistice in 1918 we who lived in or near London suffered from sporadic air raids. They never frightened me, probably because I never saw the results of aerial bombardment by high explosive (as I did in the Second World

War). But I do remember the nights made sleepless by the roar and boom of anti-aircraft fire. It became an unwritten law that you could be technically late for school, but not in any way punished for it if there had been an air raid the night before.

I only remember one occasion when there was an air raid while I was actually in school. The hall was filled for the school play, which would mean that rather more than five hundred people were there. We had reached the end of the first act (the play was, I think, that evergreen *Dandy Dick*), the stage lights were off and only a few glimmering gas jets lighted the auditorium which was partially blacked out. Suddenly came the shrilling of air wardens' whistles, and their continued cries of "Take cover!" The anti-aircraft guns had just begun their usual racket and a panic in that crowded hall could easily have started.

However, as if on cue, the figure of our headmaster appeared before the stage curtains with a spotlight focused on him. He was a commanding figure at any time, and now he seemed super-human in his dignity and icy calm. "Steady, School!" he said, clearly but not very loudly, and at once the murmurs of incipient panic died down. "There is no immediate danger, but I want you all to disperse to the form rooms."

It was a masterly display of control, for within minutes the whole gathering had quietly dispersed with the headmaster's instructions about exactly where each two or three rows should go. No doubt the possibility of an air raid on a dark autumn night had occurred to him previously, and he had some time beforehand planned exactly what he would do. Nevertheless the clockwork precision with which the manoeuvre was carried out impresses me to this day. We spent an hour or more in various form rooms singing patriotic songs until the All Clear sounded, and then, seeing that the hour was late, went home.

The headmaster, Shirley Goodwin by name, had all the qualities needed by a good head. I looked on him with awe from the first, but later when he personally taught us the Greek and Roman Classics which he knew and loved so well my awe turned into respect, admiration, and even deep affection.

School sports

At first I was actually embarrassed by not being able to play "rugger". For some reason I did not feel able to say that it was a matter of doctor's orders, and I felt shy about confessing to the weakness of double pneumonia only a few weeks before. However, apart from a little good-natured ragging for being a "cissy" I was left alone until the next term when I took my place in the house third fifteen. I almost always enjoyed rugger, though I don't think I was ever very skilful. Still, that is surely one of the game's great merits. You can work off a good deal of energy, even of aggression, and generally enjoy yourself without any particular skill.

The times when I grew to dread the game were when the weather was very bad and the ground excessively muddy and sticky. It is not in the least that I minded getting muddied all over, but that the changing facilities were primitive in the extreme. During the war, and for some years afterwards, there was no hot water, and for us juniors there were no baths. Washing had to be done, as I said, in cold water in hand-basins. This was an awkward and messy process, and I must say that I was considerably relieved when, perhaps through snow or fog, the game was cancelled.

Again, partly through the total lack of young men on the staff, no one actually taught us the game. Of course from time to time the older boys would give us hints, but on the whole we picked up the game and its rules and practices as we went along. It would probably be true to say that I have learnt more about how the game should be played by watching it many years later on T.V., and listening to an expert commentator, than I ever learned in my years of actually playing.

Cricket was compulsory, and how I loathed it. If I were batting I was usually out in the first over or two; I could not bowl, and was usually sent somewhere near the boundary to field. I evidently could not be relied on to make a sure catch or make a swift and effective return. I thus came to the conclusion that cricket is only a good and enjoyable game for those who have some talent for it. This has remained my opinion.

About this time the point was brought home to me that "having an eye for the ball" had little to do with possessing good eyesight. I knew boys at school whose eyesight was definitely poor but who had this magical power of co-ordination of hand and eye. Later, at Cambridge, I found the same thing was true. Young men who had to wear glasses for reading were first-class performers at such things as hockey and cricket. Yet I knew my eyesight was very good. The very first time I was allowed to use live ammunition on the school's twenty-five yard miniature range I scored six bulls out of six at a stationary target with no trouble at all. The whole thing still remains a bit of a mystery to me.

Apart from cricket, the only other physical thing I dreaded at school was swimming. I always hated and feared water, more particularly as I was always shivering with cold. The school swimming bath was not heated, and for a skinny little boy these weekly sessions were sheer purgatory. Again, the staff shortage was partly responsible. All we had by way of an instructor was a retired sergeant-major who had run to fat. He never entered the water, but paced up and down the bath's side, shouting loud, but to me incomprehensible, instructions. The same fat, loud-voiced character took us for what was laughingly called "gym". I can't remember learning anything whatever from him except to be quick on the word of command.

Travel in London

During all my years at Emanuel I do not remember missing a single day through ill health. Every day I had to walk, whatever the weather, to Mortlake station, take the train to Clapham Junction and then walk a further mile or so to Emanuel School. I did not particularly mind this, but I cannot help comparing my lot with the grammar school children of today, who are in many cases brought by motor coach more or less from door to door.

Of course in those days we had fog, sometimes of the "peasouper" variety. I found this exciting, for you could very easily get lost, at least temporarily, and the train services, usually most reliable, were seriously disrupted. Familiar streets were shrouded in mystery and such traffic as there was moved at a cautious snail's pace. One moved in a strangely

41

quiet, dark world and in some way the time sense was temporarily in abeyance. Certainly no one expected you to be punctual under the conditions of London fog.

I feel I must pay tribute to the excellent service of the electric trains of the (then) London and South Western Railway – before long to be merged into the "Southern". They were punctual and, except in case of fog, absolutely reliable. I only remember one case of a breakdown, and that was quickly remedied. The train was heavily overcrowded and as we moved off the main fuse blew with a noise like that of a small bomb going off and the eerie green light of melting and exploding copper. This fuse was none of your fiddly little bits of tin or tinned copper wire such as we meet in our houses. It was a broad thickish band of copper mounted between the shoe which collected the current from the live rail and the control box of the driver. This fuse was designed to blow at 900 amperes and since the voltage at which the train operated was about 600 the resulting explosion of energy was not insignificant. The sudden conversion of 540 thousand watts into heat was a sight, and a sound, to be remembered. Imagine 540 bars of an ordinary electric fire suddenly disintegrating with explosive heat and you will see what I mean. In the event, the fuse was replaced with very little fuss, and the overloaded train proceeded, albeit cautiously, on its way.

Electric motors

This reliable electric train service further supplied us in frosty weather with a glorious pyrotechnic exhibition of terrific sparks and flashes as the connecting shoes made uncertain contact with the icy live rail.

Nevertheless, I was bothered, really bothered, by the fact that no one could tell me how an electric motor *worked*. Just how did this invisible force turn electric motors and pull along trains loaded with hundreds of people? My father, the most untechnically minded man I ever met, had naturally no idea, and my school friends neither knew nor cared. It must be remembered that domestic appliances which contained electric motors, such as vacuum cleaners, food mixers and fans were unknown in our circles in, say, 1920. Otherwise I would

42

soon have dismantled one and found out. Toys, electrical or otherwise, did not appear for some years after the First World War, and all I had to speculate about was the *appearance* of a small electric motor illustrated in a pre-war catalogue from Gamages, the big general store in Holborn. (Incidentally, during the war years I used to spend hours of useless longing over this catalogue. A stationary steam engine was four shillings and elevenpence; a clockwork train set, consisting of an engine, tender, two coaches and a set of rails was the same price; even the magical, and utterly unobtainable, electric motor was only a few shillings more. Alas, such fairy-tale prices were never to return.)

Of course in due time, and after many abortive experiments, I did find out quite a lot about electric motors, dynamos and many other things. But I think my agony of mind at *not knowing* would have been considerably cut short if I had proceeded to study physics. But someone in authority decided that I showed promise in Latin and Greek. Just before my mother died in the autumn of 1921, I was removed to what was called the Classical IVth and I was taken clean away from science and plunged into the Greek and Roman world with a little relief in the realm of English literature.

3

Adolescent Struggles
1921–1925

Boys are much more sensitive and much more imaginative than we are sometimes disposed to believe. Their toughness and noisiness are very often not much more than a defence for their own growing personalities. We must never forget, therefore, that we are dealing with highly sensitive material . . . The real truth of the matter is that boys are emerging from the stage, not many years ago, when they were dependent upon their mothers, and they are moving forward towards the stage of real independence.

The stepmother

I don't propose to deal in any depth with the emotional effect of my mother's tragic death. I felt I had lost my greatest friend and in a sense my home. I had now no great incentive to work, and I think I must in fairness give credit to the school itself for carrying me on without despair and overmuch bitterness. Domestically we were cared for (as far as basic essentials were concerned) by another domestic treasure by the name of Rhoda, and all three of us owe her a great debt. We saw almost nothing of our grief-stricken father, and we certainly had no idea that before many months had passed he was considering marriage to his six foot-two-inch wartime secretary.

I sometimes think that my stepmother did far more emotional harm than she could possibly have realised. We three were perfectly normal, reasonably happy children, and, though still suffering from the loss of our mother, were quite prepared to co-operate with a mother-substitute. Our stepmother had been a fairly frequent visitor to the house and had always treated us with courtesy and a rather reserved kindness. But the moment she became my father's wife she changed instantly into a terrifying kill-joy. There was nothing with which she did not find fault. If one said nothing at table one was accused of being sullen, but if we did pluck up courage to speak we were nearly always shot down in flames – though perhaps that is an inappropriate phrase to use to describe her gelid replies. She was the conversation-stopper of all time. I cannot remember any guests coming to the house, and I must say I am not surprised.

My brother was sent to St. Lawrence College, Ramsgate (a real public school in my stepmother's eyes) while I continued at Emanuel, with the promise that I should go to Cambridge later. My sister went to Westfield College (part of London University) to study for her B.Sc. It seemed to me at the time that I had to put up with more than my share of my stepmother's rudeness and frigidity. I can remember once saying casually, "Well, I think I'll go up to my room now." Back came the freezing reply, "It's not *your* room, John" (she insisted on calling me this though everyone else called me Jack), "it is the room I allow you to use!" This was wounding enough, but we found out that little by little all our childhood treasures disappeared, including anything that could remind us of our mother. When we arrived home for the holidays the first question was, "Well, how long is it this time?" and the chill of unwelcome lay over everything. My stepmother cared nothing for our health (thank God we were healthy naturally) and it is not without significance that I had never been to a dentist until I was twenty-one. After all, no schoolboy or undergraduate is going to bother unless he has toothache. But the mother-substitute might I feel have shown a little concern.

Thus, from the age of almost fifteen I had in effect no real home. Fortunately I had many friends, and various interests such as dramatics and debating. Model aeroplane-making and other activities began to add to my interests at school. Since under my stepmother's regime to be five minutes late meant no dinner at all in the evening, I must, two or three times a week, have survived on such things as chocolate bars and potato crisps. I can't think now how I ever managed even this, for my pocket money was still only a few pence a week. But I was fit and full of energy as well as of ideas, despite the meagre diet.

Wireless

From the age of sixteen life began to be a battle against poverty. Wireless broadcasting began about 1921 and I was "in" it almost from the first. Even to get the most primitive equipment I had to scrimp and scrape, and haunt the shops which were now beginning to sell war surplus electrical goods. Necessity is indeed the mother of invention and the inventive ingenuities to which I was driven by sheer lack of cash would make a laughable, if not boring, catalogue. It was not long before I was receiving London (2LO) on a cheaply acquired pair of ex-army headphones.

But my heart was set on acquiring a valve (tube in America). You can't amplify with a crystal; all you can do is to de-code the broadcast signal. But a valve opened all kinds of magic possibilities. You could magnify the signal's strength by ten or even twenty and hear foreign stations which were up till then inaudible on the headset. You might even make the local signal loud enough to be heard on a loudspeaker – if you had a loudspeaker. But valves, even the cheapest Dutch ones, were dear, and ten shillings was the lowest price I ever saw one marked at.

Thus began the Great Dinner Ticket Racket. My father paid for a term's school dinners in advance. (Incidentally I always felt ashamed as I presented his cheque. Why couldn't we pay with real money, like everyone else?) The dinners were quite good, though rather slapdash in their cooking and serving, and I discovered that there were boys anxious to eat them. I therefore began what I suppose was a sort of black market in dinner tickets. It is true that I rarely got the fair market price and usually had to be content with tenpence or even eight-pence, in exchange for my shilling ticket. I knew very well that I could exist quite happily on a bar or two of chocolate especially if I knew that I would be home on time for my stepmother's dinner. On and off, then, for the next period of nearly two years, I hoarded every penny of my ill-gotten gains, and was thus able to buy one or two essentials for my wireless career. It often meant walking several miles to find the recommended junk-shop, but I didn't mind that. My experiments were backed by almost no theoretical knowledge, but you can learn a lot by trial and error. Apart from my school work, which I did just well enough to escape censure, my whole energy went into the wireless craze. I remember one school report which stated baldly, "Good, but rather too much wireless."

The first publications

Somewhere about this time I wrote two articles for the popular "wireless" press, and what is more I was paid two guineas for each of them. In that curious world of mingled enthusiasm and ignorance, when millions were building their own receivers, I probably knew neither more nor less than the average fan. It was just lucky for me that I could write about some of the problems we encountered. I remember one of these precious cheques arriving by the evening post (yes, we had an evening delivery in those days) and having to listen to a boring little lecture from my ever-cautious father. "You'll never earn your living by writing, my boy!' he declared solemnly. At that time I had no idea of so doing, but the years that were to come proved him wrong.

If you are bored by matters of wireless or electricity then by all means skip the next few paragraphs. I include them because I honestly believe that the exercise of extreme ingenuity and the hundreds of hours of concentration on experiments kept me sane and almost free from brooding about the grievous loss of my mother and the then dictatorial regime. To her credit let it be said that my stepmother never once interfered with my electrical experiments (some of which were indeed dangerous).

Experiments

Our house was fed by direct current (D.C.). This is now hardly existent anywhere, as the whole country is fed, via the national grid, with alternating current (A.C.). But it had its advantages. You can, for instance, charge an accumulator direct from the mains via a resistance to drop the voltage. In my case this consisted of one or more carbon filament light bulbs, contributed by my mother's sisters. To the end of their lives (after the Second World War) they continued to use carbon filament bulbs, in such places as the "smallest room", in the erroneous belief that because they gave little light they used little current.

Early in the experiments I discovered that our "positive" in the electric sense was "earth". The metal plate which I had laboriously buried as an earth for my crystal set was in fact the ferocious source of all our electrical energy. How the *earth* could be *positive* caused me much puzzlement, and it was years before I learned how this could be so; at the time there was no one to tell me.

Well, anyway, here I was with a supply of direct current at 200 volts and a few carbon filament bulbs. (Incidentally by using the stout earth wire of the wireless set I discovered that I was bypassing the meter. But this theft of electric current, largely unintentional, could not have cost the Company, as it then was, more than a few pence.)

The accumulator

The next thing I needed was an accumulator (or storage battery) which could be charged, used and re-charged with little trouble. I could not possibly afford to buy one, and I proceeded to *make* one. Sheet celluloid was not too difficult to obtain and celluloid can easily be joined together by a sticky cement made by dissolving scraps of celluloid in amyl acetate. So much for the case. I then had the good luck to find a shop which sold the lead plates and wooden separators at a reasonable price. Having got the plates, I then had to solder them together in pairs. I was not then skilled in soldering and my father's outsize soldering-iron did not make the job any easier. However, finally it was done, and a friendly local chemist sold me the needed sulphuric acid of the proper specific gravity. And *it worked*. There is nothing like overcoming seemingly insuperable difficulties to fill one with a sense of triumph.

Electrical machine gun

Fortunately in the 1920s copper was not the semi-precious metal it has since become, and copper-wire in all reasonable gauges was cheap and easy to come by. I was thus able to make all sorts of experiments in magnetism, the most spectacular of which was what would be called today a "linear accelerator" electric motor. I used a series of windings around a disused clinical thermometer tube (the only tube I could lay hands on) and by switching them on and off in rapid succession I propelled a half-inch Meccano steel rod at such speed that it shot across the room like a bullet and imbedded itself in the door! I felt I had proved my point – that such an affair as a machine gun need not depend on a noisy, and flashy, series of explosions. But I did not repeat that particular experiment again. It was only too obviously lethal.

Wireless from the mains

I made a crude electric arc furnace in which copper could easily be melted. The light from the incandescent carbon rods was excruciatingly bright and I had no goggles. Later I combined what little I knew about electricity with my small knowledge of wireless. I think I must have been among the first to run a wireless set from the mains. The results were far from perfect, for although D.C. does not suffer from the typical A.C. "hum" it is not a completely pure flow of current. It suffers from what is called "commutator ripple" and the resultant signal in the headphones or loudspeaker always contains this background of ripple. I did not then know how this could be cured, although in fact the remedy is simple enough.

Finally I made a loudspeaker. The components were an American earphone (made for someone, I thought, with exceptionally large ears), a cow's horn and a rather battered speaking trumpet. All these were bought for a few shillings at various junk-shops. I used plaster of Paris as a base, subsequently enamelled to a smart black, and the various parts of the horn were bolted together. And, joy of joys, it worked.

The only original discovery I ever made during these two or three years was that tuning coils could be made far more efficient by using a core of iron-dust, and that they could be "tuned" by moving the core in and out. I used iron-dust "lifted" from the school chemistry laboratory and bound it together with shellac varnish. I find it interesting to reflect that there is hardly a radio or television set made anywhere in the world today that does not rely on the movement of an iron-dust "slug" for its tuning at higher frequencies. But of course the whole business is far more accurate and technologically advanced than my early discovery of the 1920s.

School

Meantime, you may well ask, what was happening at school? Well I was working, but not too strenuously. I loved the Classics especially Homer and Horace but I must say that I got bored by the interminable history of Thucydides. I suffered two "double removes", being once lifted from the Classical IVth before my time and then to the Classical VIth. I say that I suffered these quick promotions because they were not popular with my contemporaries (though I made no enemies) nor with the teaching staff who thought I needed to be made, or kept, humble. In fact I do not think that I was at that time in the least conceited; in fact I was bewildered by the mysterious brilliance which I was supposed to possess. I was much more in need of reassurance than taking down.

O.T.C.

Before I turn to my last and happiest year at school, I must briefly mention the O.T.C. (Officers Training Corps). To join this was quite voluntary, but I joined rather reluctantly since the military world was quite foreign to me. But before long, and despite such abominable chores as winding puttees round my legs, I quite enjoyed myself. Even square-bashing which included the proper handling of a rifle appealed to me. We aimed at no less than perfection in discipline and rhythm of movement and I can't say I ever found this boring.

On field days we joined with other London day schools such as St. Paul's and the City of London School, and skirmished among the trees and bracken of Richmond Park with blank cartridges. I remember that St. Paul's had a reputation for using rabbit droppings for bullets, while we were strictly forbidden to put anything down the barrels of our rifles. The object of the exercises, and who, if anyone, won, remains a mystery to me. But I must have enjoyed the good company of my friends in the O.T.C. for I went three times to the annual training camp for school O.T.C.s at Tidworth or some similar military base. In my last year I had become a school prefect, head of my house and a sergeant in the O.T.C.

Shirley Goodwin

In the Classical VIth we were taught more often than not by our revered headmaster, Balliol scholar and perfect gentleman, Shirley Goodwin, and it was through his enthusiasm that at last the Classics came alive. I don't say that our head was very good at teaching us to pass exams, but his real love for Greek and Latin infected us all. In particular he taught me to translate. He hated "translator's" English as though it was the devil himself. It was quite usual for us to spend a full hour in translating one verse of an ode of the Latin poet Horace. And this had to be done into English verse. This did nothing to improve my Latin or Greek grammar or syntax, but it filled me with the enthusiasm which began its fruition some seventeen years later.

Cambridge

I had been accepted at Emmanuel College, Cambridge as a promising student of Classics, and my father believed that I should win a county scholarship, and thus help to raise the wind. To do this one had to reach a certain standard in the Higher School Certificate (roughly equivalent to today's A levels). To my dismay and to his great annoyance I failed, just, to reach the qualifying standard. The "stiff letter" was of course sent to my headmaster, who had assured my father that my work was up to scholarship standard, but nothing ever came of this.

So I went up to Cambridge as a poor man's son, as my father was quick to point out. I can't think now how I managed. The total amount available for my first year which began in October 1924 (when I was barely eighteen) was £180. Out of this I was allowed ten shillings a week pocket money, but this had to pay for my lunch in "digs", and I was unable to join many social activities because of sheer lack of money. I had a raincoat but no overcoat and very little more than the clothes I stood up in. Although I was glad enough to be up at Cambridge, that first year caused me much financial misery and embarrassment.

Of course I can see now that I was sent up to Cambridge a year (at least) too early. Another year at school would have filled in the gaps in my knowledge of Latin and Greek and undoubtedly have made the scholarship a probability. Moreover, I should have had a year's more experience of life and perhaps acquired the good sense of really getting down to the discipline of work at once, instead of largely wasting my time in the giddy atmosphere of almost total freedom.

In the first year I attended a few lectures and did enough translation work and other Classical reading to keep my tutor relatively happy. He was L. G. H. Greenwood, a first-class scholar from New Zealand, and he treated me fairly and kindly. Only once did he reprimand me, and that was when I failed my Mays (a sort of trial run for the Tripos examination the following year). I don't remember his words, except that they were few, but he certainly reminded me that I was not really using such potential as I had.

Christian influences

I went up to Cambridge as an avowed atheist, and I don't think I ever attended college chapel. But, as is almost inevitable, I was before long approached by members of both the Student Christian Movement and of that formidable evangelical group called the Cambridge Intercollegiate Christian Union. I can remember attending meetings of both societies, and felt strangely attracted by some members of the CICCU. I had never met men before to whom Christ was a living reality, as real as any human friend. Their certainty about God, their utter personal devotion to Christ and their willingness to go to any lengths to win someone else to Christ could hardly fail to impress a very young-for-his-age eighteen year old.

But I resisted membership of the Christian Union for some

months. I could not understand their ban on smoking, on cinema or theatre-going or indeed on any worldly pleasure. In sober fact I was abstaining from even the most innocent of worldly pleasures, for the simple reason that I could not afford any of them. But the puritanical insistence on abstention from anything that the "world" offered in the way of pleasure or amusement was something I found very hard to take; and still do.

4

Destined for the Ministry
1925–1930

What is it, for example, that lives within the spirit of a man
which enables him to detect truth, even though it may
prove painful and destructive to his previous illusions?
Here lies one of life's great mysteries. What God-given
faculty is it that enables us to recognise the Word of God as
the Word of God and not as a mere human opinion or doctrine?

Return to Christian faith

What finally led me back to the path of Christianity is a
longish story. But a significant point in my pilgrimage happened in the spring of 1925. My father and stepmother had
tired of suburbia and were building a house at Woldingham,
nearly 900 feet up on the Surrey North Downs. They might
have guessed, but did not, that the house would not be ready
on time. Consequently the Easter vacation found us three
without anywhere to stay. (My father and stepmother were
living at the post office in Woldingham, and indeed stayed
there for several months.) My sister was by this time a student
at Westfield College, London, and among her friends was a
girl whose father was rector of two out-of-the-way village
churches in north Devon. He and his wife very kindly allowed
the three of us children to stay as paying guests, and we were
very happy. I had never seen Devon lanes in spring, with their
steep grassy sides almost entirely covered with untold
thousands of primroses. Always sensitive to beauty I was
almost overwhelmed by the sheer loveliness of all that I saw. I

walked for miles, mostly by myself, almost literally intoxi-
cated by the sounds and scents and vistas which were all
around me.

The Cambridge term was shorter than the London one; and
shorter too than the school term at St. Lawrence, Ramsgate,
where my brother had been sent a year or so before. So that I
was already half-drunk with the beauties of nature when my
sister and her college friend arrived. I fell almost instantly in
love with this girl. I don't think for a moment that I was ever in
love with her in the true sense, but the sheer beauty of that
spring added to my own loneliness of spirit produced in me all
the well known symptoms of a very young man in love. It was
gorgeous to be alive. This girl and I used to walk and talk a lot
together, and before long I discovered that she had much the
same spiritual outlook as the CICCU. She even asked me
bluntly, "Are you a Christian?" And I was at a loss to know
how to reply.

Anyway, on my return to Cambridge I began to think that
this way, narrow though it seemed to be, produced some very
fine and attractive people. I began to attend the daily prayer
meeting, held in the Henry Martyn Hall in Cambridge, and to
go to the evening service held after evensong in Holy Trinity
Church. (The vicar at that time was E. S. Woods, soon to be
Bishop of Croydon.) For these Sunday gatherings prominent
evangelical preachers were invited from far and wide and,
although I was often puzzled and sometimes disagreed, I had
never heard such fervent and persuasive preaching in my life.
Although I had been brought up to treat the scriptures with
reverence, I had never before met men to whom the Bible was
the Word of God, the actual means through which the living
God spoke to men. I could not fail to be very impressed and
before long, although without any "conversion" experience, I
joined the Christian Union – with certain reservations which
persisted throughout my Cambridge days.

University life

Meanwhile, in my ordinary college life I worked, in mod-
eration, and made many friends. As has been said many times
before, the real educational value of a university lies not

merely in its lectures and tutorials but in the informal social contacts where discussion is free and uninhibited. At school, once we had the privilege of the house prefects' study, we used to talk and talk about every issue under the sun. At Cambridge the same thing happened, on a more informed and intelligent level. Surely this will always be so when young and lively minds meet together. I could not afford to join the University Union, and the college debating society struck me as rather stiff and formal, its speeches aimed more at scoring points of debate than at getting at the truth. Possibly I am unfair over this, but I do know how much I learned in the completely informal getting together of friends and the un-limited argument and discussion of almost all that we knew about life. Strangely enough, as I look back at all this miscel-laneous barrage of words, I can hardly remember any serious political discussion.

Keswick

In July of 1925 I was persuaded to attend the Keswick Convention. This week, which had been held for many years previously, was intended for the "deepening of the spiritual life", and some 5,000 people assembled for Bible readings and addresses in the Big Tent. How they were accommodated in the little town of Keswick I do not know, but we had our own Cambridge camp under canvas, only a few hundred yards from the main centre of activities. I had never seen the beauties of the Lake District before and my senses were overwhelmed by my first sight of real mountains and real lakes. And I could hardly fail to be impressed by the Big Tent, packed day after day by earnest, but by no means joyless Christians. The hymn singing was moving, the prayers were offered in touching sincerity, and the speakers spoke with what seemed to me great power. I cannot honestly say that I took in much from them, but it was almost literally Heaven to find oneself, with the girl I felt I so deeply loved, among so many people who, despite their funny little taboos, were plainly devoted to Jesus Christ. I was enormously exhilarated and felt that I really must, decisively, throw in my lot with these lovable devoted people.

Back in Cambridge in October, now that I knew that I had failed my Mays I began to work in earnest at the Classics. I was horribly hampered by certain blanks of sheer ignorance in matters of both Latin and Greek grammar and syntax. This was at least partly due to poor teaching at school. I was too shy to ask, and my tutor was too much of a gentleman to probe into gaps in my basic knowledge. The small group with whom I worked were largely from St. Paul's School, London, and I can remember marvelling at their thorough familiarity with Latin and Greek. Very occasionally I summoned up courage to ask for their help.

As I have hinted before, I was never good at ball games, but I discovered at Cambridge that, being light and fit, I could run a half-mile in a reasonable time, and that anything up to eight or ten miles I could keep going a great deal better than most. Training was pretty severe; running six to nine miles almost every day must always be hard work. But I can still remember that glowing feeling of fitness that comes upon one when the training is complete. I did nothing distinguished apart from occasionally running for my college at the half-mile, but enjoyed my athletic career.

Caricatures

During my second year at Cambridge I discovered my talent for caricature, or rather re-discovered it, for I had occasionally drawn caricatures for the school magazine. Many a dull lecture was enlivened, I think, by my passing round a malicious caricature of the lecturer. Before long I found I was drawing pretty regularly for the undergraduate magazine *Granta*. This led sometimes to a free pass to some theatrical shows, or to a favoured position from which to view a distinguished visitor. (One of these, I remember, was G. K. Chesterton, who was a "gift" to any caricaturist.) Once only was I invited to attend the editorial conference, to discuss a special Victorian number which we were planning. I can vividly remember Hugh Herklots, J. E. Sewell, and Geoffrey Gorer, and others just as witty and amusing. I think that all that company have since distinguished themselves in various arts – reviewing, editing, stage producing, novel writing, and film production. Among those young men I experienced that peculiar thrill at being "in conference" with those whose gifts and ability to think were much better and quicker than my own. It gives me the deepest possible pleasure to see the instant understanding that first-class brains can give each other – and the enormous amount of time saved thereby.

I can remember, apart from drawing for *Granta*, doing some much larger pen-and-wash-coloured cartoons. One of my victims was J. T. Sheppard, then provost of Kings. These efforts of mine were duly hung at the summer exhibition of the Cambridge art society. Just above my offerings was a large black-and-white self-portrait of Cecil Beaton. The thing that I chiefly remember was that part of the "shading" of the back hair was formed by repeated rubber-stamping saying, "Good old Cecil Beaton!"

Father Trout

At some time during the summer of 1926 a great, and indeed fundamental change came over my life. We were living, as I have said, on the North Downs in Surrey. Life at home was unhappy and, since we had no car, we were very isolated. But less than a couple of miles away there lived a clergyman whom we will call Father Trout. He had many faults but he was essentially a very kindly man. He was, I suppose, about sixty years old at the time, and had worked in commerce of some kind before becoming ordained in the Church of England. More importantly perhaps he had given many years' service to the Cambridge University mission to boys in Bermondsey. He genuinely loved these boys, and in fact adopted two of them and had them educated at his own expense.

It so happened that my brother Ken became very friendly with one of these adopted sons, Harold, at St. Lawrence College. Harold invited my brother to spend the next school holidays at Father Trout's house, and very soon my brother became one of the regular gang who lived there. It was not long before I exchanged the unwelcoming atmosphere of home for a place where, although there was a strict evangelical atmosphere, there was much love, affection, friendship, laughter and gaiety. I was made instantly welcome, and my brother got on so well with the reverend Father that a future at Cambridge seemed assured for him after all.

At the time to which I am referring Father Trout was semi-retired, lived in a largish house and had several young fellows staying with him. I did not know this at the time, but he was running a fairly informal course in Bible study for those whom he thought would one day become missionaries, parsons or at least teachers of the Christian faith. He must, of course, have had some money of his own, but he ran very successfully a fund for training men according to evangelical standards. He had a great charm of personality and I don't think he found it over-difficult to persuade rich old ladies to make him generous gifts. At least by supporting his fund they would be ensuring that the Church of England would have some real faithful-to-the-Bible clergymen.

Father Trout welcomed not only me and my brother but my sister also to spend our vacations at his house. The sense of welcome was tremendous, and the presence of some seven or eight other young men was invigorating. There were no luxuries in that house, which became my home in vacation-time for the next three years, but we were well fed and made to feel wanted. Every evening we had at least an hour and a half's Bible reading, led by Father Trout himself. He was no ready speaker, but neither was he boring, and I quite enjoyed a steady diet of the Epistles of the New Testament. When, in later years, I was to translate these same epistles into *Letters to Young Churches* I was grateful indeed for those long hours of intensive study. Father Trout was no scholar (indeed it was commonly said that he only knew two words of Greek and one of these he habitually mispronounced) but he had a comprehensive grasp of the whole of the Authorised Version, and he could make it come alive for us.

Every Sunday he would take us all, in an enormous Sunbeam tourer, to evening worship at some church of his choice. His churchmanship was of the lowest protestant order. Bowing at the name of Jesus in the Creed was forbidden, and he did not really approve of the singing of the responses – a custom I had accepted since childhood. I have called him

"Father" Trout deliberately because although he would have instantly repudiated such an Anglo-Catholic title his whole attitude was so paternal, so patriarchal indeed, that one could think of him in no other way.

Apart from offering me a home for the vacations, Father Trout also assisted me financially. He was genuinely disturbed that I should be living in such poverty and immediately offered me fifty pounds a year to help. Almost at the same time I was awarded belatedly a Leaving Exhibition of fifty pounds from my school, so, although I still had to live very carefully, I was not, from then on, so utterly poverty-stricken as I had been.

As one looks back on a rather odd situation I think that, apart from real compassion, the good Father Trout knew that my sister intended to serve as a missionary in India, and that my brother was beginning to feel a call to work in China. Indeed probably, he saw me as a possible candidate for ordination, but certainly he did not mention the matter to me for over a year.

Reading English

Despite my endeavours I only managed to gain third class honours in Classics. After some discussion it was decided that I should read for the English Tripos in my remaining year. This is really a two-year course but it was thought that I could get a reasonable degree if I worked hard. My tutor was the redoubtable F. R. Leavis, who advised me to attend very few lectures but to read as much as I could in the library of the English school. Leavis reminded me that the course really included almost the whole of English literature, and gave me some wise advice about what periods I should concentrate on. "You're bound to get some questions on these," he said; and he was right.

My last year at Cambridge was a very happy one. I spent long hours in reading anything I could lay hands on in the English library, with Dr. Leavis' recommendations in mind. Apart from the demands made on my time by the CICCU I used to go out sketching in water-colours, and continued my cartoon work for *Granta* from time to time. I was also able, very occasionally, to go to concerts and can chiefly remember the visit of that distinguished trio, Cortot, Thibaud and Casals, and to this day I can remember almost by heart their matchless rendering of Schubert's Trio in B flat.

I continued to attend the Keswick Convention during my three years at Cambridge, although I must confess that it was the magical beauty of the scenery and the good fellowship of the camp which mostly attracted me. Perhaps I was, as in other things, a slow developer but although I listened attentively to the convention speakers I cannot today recollect anything of what they said, and I can hardly remember the general drift of their argument. But they certainly continued to convey a sense of the living-ness of Christ, and of the necessity to be guided by Him throughout the life that, for me, lay mostly in the future.

Let me not be unfair to the Keswick Convention. I am sure that it has been, and is, a spiritual refreshment and tonic to the large numbers who attend it, perhaps most of all to the missionaries who come on furlough from lonely and difficult parts of the world. I think it was my own immaturity that mostly prevented me from reaping more than marginal benefits.

Children's Special Service Mission (CSSM)

Each summer I, with many other members of the Christian Union, used to help run a seaside mission under the auspices of the Children's Special Service Mission. It was great fun for the most part; I have the happiest memories of fellow-workers and children at Overstrand, Cromer and Eastbourne. But in those days it was a real ordeal to me to speak in public, especially from a sand or shingle "pulpit", probably with a strong breeze blowing. The audience were a few hundred lively youngsters and the critics, the parents and others who leant on promenade rails to listen.

Prayer answered

One particular personal incident remains in my mind, and I think it deserves to be recorded. It was at Overstrand, a delightful village in Norfolk, and I was a young nineteen year old with a newly acquired faith of an almost literal kind. The promises of God recorded in the Bible were true and meant to be apprehended by any believer. Thus it was that, in that dreadful year of poverty, I found myself almost literally penniless, and certainly unable any longer to pay the very modest fees of our mission houseparty. I was wandering on the beach one evening and I suddenly thought, Christ said, "Ask and it shall be given you," so why not ask? So I did, with simple naive childlike faith, and within two minutes I saw an unusually bright sparkle shining on a bank of shingle in the setting sun. I ran forward and picked up a ring with a very large sapphire mounted on it. On my way back to the house in which we were staying I had to visit the village post office. And there, for everyone to see, was a large notice offering "£20 reward for the recovery of a valuable sapphire ring." My heart leapt in thankfulness and I went straight to the hotel of the owner of the ring. Needless to say he was delighted, and on hearing that I intended to give half the reward to the mission, he unhesitatingly increased it. It must have been a very valuable sapphire indeed, but much more valuable to me was the fact that God Himself had heard my desperate prayer and had immediately answered it. I have had many answers to prayer since but none so rapid and demonstrable.

Sherborne

As the summer of 1927 drew on I had some discussion with one or two in authority in college as well as with various trusted friends as to what I should do in the future. Influenced no doubt by the enthusiastically evangelical atmosphere which I had been breathing for some terms I had a vague idea of going to Africa as an educational missionary. I had a very shadowy idea at that time of becoming a parson. I managed to get second class honours in English, but was not allowed to receive my B.A. degree since I was not yet twenty-one. (I have already said that I went up to Cambridge too early.) My friends who thought I might one day end up as a priest in the Church of England pointed out that I could not be ordained until the age of twenty-three. It seemed sensible to put in a year, or perhaps two, at prep school teaching. Armed only with a glowing and not-too-well deserved testimonial from my Classics tutor, Mr. Greenwood (to whom I owe so much) I succeeded at once in my application to join the staff of Sherborne Preparatory School.

I fell in love with Sherborne almost at first sight, and I still love the place. Naturally I did not for a moment think then that I should be re-visiting it again and again some thirty years later when my daughter was a pupil at Sherborne School for Girls. At the age of not quite twenty-one it seemed to me all that a small town should be, complete with a magnificent abbey and surrounded (as it still is) by the most ravishingly unspoilt countryside.

I had an ancient motor bike and on this I explored the really glorious county of Dorset. I can never forget its beauty and can still remember being literally shaken and almost violently sick when I returned for the summer term and saw the magnificent banners of early summer shouting with joy on every hand.

Although I had never been a schoolmaster before I found no difficulty in teaching. I think it is part of my innate passion for communication that makes it easy for me to help others to absorb knowledge. I don't know how good I was at getting the boys to pass their Common Entrance for in the event I only stayed at Sherborne for one year. But I do remember that I had no trouble about discipline. The boys I taught were interested and even enthusiastic over, for example, a hitherto unknown subject such as Greek.

I did my school work conscientiously but I let myself in for several extra mural activities. I used to preach for various local parsons in their village churches; to address a men's Bible class on many Sunday afternoons, and to run (very badly) a club for the working-class boys of the town.

Among the many memories of that crowded and, on the whole, very happy year, two particular incidents stand out in my mind. One was concerned with scouting. I was more or less expected to be assistant scoutmaster, and I well recollect crawling through the undergrowth in a copse about a mile away from the school. The memory is that of an almost deafening chorus of nightingale song. I had always thought that the nightingale was a solitary bird and only sang at night. But not in that copse near Sherborne.

The other memory is concerned with my new motor bike and sidecar. (Now that I was at least earning money I could afford a decent, and fast, machine.) Well, one evening at dinner, a message was received that the cook, who was enjoying her evening off, had missed the last bus, and would I fetch her in my sidecar? Of course I would. True, it was dark, but had I not an electric headlamp? And with a fast machine the journey was negligible to me. What I had not realised was that the cook, who was a fine solid Dorset type, had never travelled fast in her life, particularly at night. So when, after some fifteen minutes of fast driving, I duly delivered her to her domestic quarters, I found she was, in modern parlance, "in shock" from the speed and noise of her journey. It took us some time to get her out of the sidecar and into her chair by the kitchen fireside. I think I was pretty selfish in those days, but the lesson did register; namely that what was great fun for me could be sheer terror to someone else. I hope I have properly remembered that since.

Although I enjoyed teaching at Sherborne it was becoming increasingly obvious (and probably not only to me) that my deeper interests lay in the work of the Church. I did not experience a vocation in any dramatic sense but I had a growing feeling that the most sensible place from which I could preach the Gospel was within the framework of the Church of England – in other words to be ordained. Although, to be fair, no direct pressure was ever exerted upon me by Father Trout, he did once let slip a remark to the effect that "we need people like you in the ministry". I thought that even if I were to teach in Africa it would be a useful piece of experience to have worked as a curate in the Church at home.

Ridley Hall

My agreement with Sherborne Prep. School was a very loose one, and no difficulty was raised in releasing me after one year's service. I promptly put my name down as a student at Ridley Hall, the most evangelical college that I knew. I had by this time grown more and more of a Protestant evangelical. I was never a particularly "churchy" type, and my emotions as I approached ordination were very mixed and not, I think, at all those of a truly dedicated ordinand. The occasion was much more a necessary process to be endured than a high moment in my spiritual life.

The principal of Ridley Hall in those days was Paul Gibson, a man of remarkable personality and insight. He was an undoubted evangelical, but much too liberal for my taste. I had more than one wordy, though quite friendly, argument with him about such things as the reliability of scripture or the reality of Christ's second coming. Lectures were pretty informal and any student could interject a remark without being thought impertinent. I remember once Paul Gibson rhapsodising about the importance of "growth". "All growth," he declared rashly, "is good." "What about cancer?" I asked, and raised considerable laughter. But Paul Gibson was far too good a Christian (and too well trained in intellect) to be annoyed by this interruption, and he went on to explain what he meant by growth. I think he meant natural development.

I am nowadays ashamed to say that I chose to take not the Cambridge ordination course, which it was normal for graduates to pass, but the general ordination examination. This meant very much less work for me since the level of examination was certainly no higher than today's A levels. In any case I wasn't much interested in Church history, the growing pattern of worship, and the development of theology – with, of course, particular reference to modernism and the higher criticism, both of which I despised and dismissed from my mind. I was a determined fundamentalist, and although I was shown much kindness by the vice-principal, E. C. Essex, and the chaplain, T. G. Stuart-Smith (who later became a bishop), nothing would penetrate my rigid theology.

I was disappointed in my return to Cambridge. Somehow I thought that my original youthful dreams would return, but, of course, they never did. I was frankly bored by the lectures I attended and the books I felt bound to read. Paul Gibson "imported" various distinguished people for our edification (the only two whose names I can remember are Percy

Dearmer and Charles Raven) but, like Gallio, I "cared for none of these things".

I do not remember being told anything about preaching or reading the liturgy. We had one lecture on elocution from Dr. Hulbert, father of the famous comedians Jack and Claude. I think if we had taken him seriously we might have learned a lot about the importance of good diction. But he hadn't a chance. Some schoolmasters are born to be ragged, as every schoolboy knows. And we, to our shame, never gave the good doctor a chance, but pulled his leg unmercifully.

We had some practice in preaching by helping out in various local churches. Sometimes the more evangelically minded of us would hold open air meetings to proclaim the Gospel. We were probably unbelievably bad, but there was no one to tell us so.

The inventor

Wireless sets were not at that time allowed to Cambridge students on the grounds, presumably, that they would distract them from their studies. And in any case Cambridge in those days was not a good reception area for radio signals, and Sherborne proved equally difficult. But recollecting my eighteen months at Ridley Hall I do remember spending a lot of time making gramophones largely of my own design. Sound reproduction, which was indeed pretty crude in those days, became a growing passion with me, and what is nowadays called hi-fi still interests me deeply.

The deacon

All that is naturally by the way. My life pursued a fairly steady course and I was duly ordained deacon in St. Katharine's Church in London's dockland in 1930. The ordination was performed by the Bishop of Barking, acting for the Bishop of Rochester (who was, I think, indisposed). It is strange to reflect that Penge, one of London's poorer suburbs, fell within the boundaries of a largely rural diocese such as Rochester.

5

Early Tensions
1930–1935

I spent several years disbelieving in any kind of God at all and it took me quite a long time – quite a bit of hard thinking and experience of life – before I found the real God. And so I'm inclined to be patient with those who haven't yet found their way to a faith which makes sense in this day and age.

You see, when I found God, and of course, I'm finding out more and more about Him every day, I found He wasn't a bit like the sort of super-father-figure which had been shoved at me from various angles ever since childhood.

The thoughts and ideas which are suitable for one age group are quite unsuitable for another. We grow out of things just as we grow out of clothes, and new ideas take the place of old ideas. And, of course, this happens in the department of religion.

Penge: the first curacy

In the summer of 1929 I met, at Swanage where I now live, a fine man of God, whose name was Sidney Ford. How we came to meet I do not know, but it was on Swanage pier that he offered me a curacy in his parish of St. John's, Penge in south-east London. I accepted with alacrity, for here was a man of undoubted true piety, a dedicated pastor of human souls, and, important above all to me, a thoroughly sound conservative evangelical churchman.

Although I made many good friends in Penge, no one could say that it was an attractive suburb. I lived in small but comfortable digs, but there was no bathroom. Every Saturday I used to repair to the Victorian vicarage for my weekly scrub and soak.

St. John's, Penge, was a run-of-the-mill Victorian building but we had an excellent choir and an enthusiastic if not very numerous congregation. I was allowed to preach quite a lot and slowly improved. I certainly worked hard both then and for years afterwards at the technique of effective preaching. I used to write my sermons out in full, then read them aloud, make emendations, and then read them aloud again. Finally I memorised them and reduced the sermon to a series of points or headings which always accompanied me into the pulpit – though I rarely so much as glanced at them. There is one little trick which I taught myself then and which has proved invaluable ever since. It was simply to train oneself to have one (or two) alternative words to use in case one's memory failed at the moment of delivery. I would strongly recommend this little bit of technique.

Apart from the regular Sunday, and weekday, services we used to hold quite frequent open air meetings. Sometimes in darkest winter these were held in the playground of our church school, with the assistance of a large screen on which were projected coloured slides of the life of Jesus Christ. Artistically, I suppose, they were pretty terrible but they held the attention of quite large crowds. There were no microphones in those days, at least for public address, and I learnt to produce a loud and carrying voice for these occasions. This was doubly fortunate, for Sidney Ford, bless him, suffered at times from acute laryngitis. I grew fairly used to the idea that he might lose his voice quite unexpectedly and that I should have to give the address at very short notice.

Scouting

In Penge I resumed my scouting activities and we had a keen and quite successful troop. For three years I took them to summer camp in Ashburnham Park, near Battle, in Sussex.

Many years later, one of those scouts reminded me that I used to show them the strange Greek characters of the New Testament and then fascinate them by putting that exotic language into modern English. They listened and one at least began a process there that led to an archdeaconry.

It is always going to be difficult to bring religion naturally into scouting, because religion appears to deal with abstract things and unseen values and most boys see things in a concrete and practical way. But I believe that Christianity is a vital part of scout training. It may perhaps be compared with a vitamin which is very small in size compared with the rest of the food taken by the body. But just as the body will sicken and finally die without the tiny vitamin, so I believe the true spirit of scouting will grow weak and die unless it has a small but regular quantity of genuine Christianity. The strength of scouting is that it translates religion into practical terms, instead of worrying the boy by vague abstractions. He is taught such things as self-discipline, love of nature, service to others etc. in a most admirable way, but this very strength of scouting can become a most dangerous weakness. For unless the whole elaborate structure is related to God and the supreme eternal values, the time will come when the boy, grown extremely critical, will ask himself such questions as "Why should I serve my neighbour? Why should I discipline myself?" and unless there is an answer bigger than "Because scouting tells you to do so," we have not got him very far.

Visiting

Badminton, parish socials, sales of work, even jumble sales, I took more or less in my stride. The great weakness in my ministry lay in visiting. I was not at that time considering merely a friendly call or even a comforting chat. I was obsessed with the idea that every visit must include some clear declaration of the Gospel and some *ex tempore* prayer. Naturally enough, with this rigid pattern fixed in my mind, my normal friendliness with people was frozen over, and it was only by vast expenditure of nervous energy that I managed some visiting. I did not particularly mind visiting the sick or dying, for they were plainly in need and would welcome such spiritual comfort as I could offer. But my heart quailed at the thought of invading the life of a normal healthy family, who certainly had no use for the Church and would not welcome me, its very young and green representative, with anything like open arms. This shyness, or cowardice, preyed on my mind daily. By much earnest prayer and by screwing up my courage I did do *some* visiting.

Two visits stick in my mind. One was in response to an earnest request for prayer for a youngish woman whom doctors seemed unable to cure and who, I was assured, had not left her bed for over ten years. Well, of course, I went; I prayed and I even "laid hands" upon the patient. I was astonished to hear on the following day that the woman had got up soon after my visit, and had gone out shopping. It shows what a poor pastor I was in those days for I never followed up that extraordinary case.

There were some pretty grim cases of bad housing and some real poverty in the early 1930s in Penge. Some of these were very distressing but the visit that is chiefly imprinted on my mind was made to a very old lady living on a minute income but trying to care for no less than twenty-seven cats. Probably at her age she had lost some of her sense of smell, but I hadn't. Most of that visit was spent in desperate silent prayer that I should not vomit.

Ordination

I was ordained deacon in 1930, and "priested" in the same year. Apart from securing a letter of recommendation from my vicar, all I was required to do was to sit for an examination in the works of the Venerable Bede. The choice was between being examined in three books of Bede's *History* in English translation, or in one in the original Latin. I had no desire to spend money on buying books and I therefore elected for the one book in Latin. I never saw any of it until a couple of pages were put before me in this farcical examination. I knew Latin pretty well in those days and the task of translating fairly elementary Latin unseen was no trouble at all. This, apart from a few routine questions from the Bishop's chaplain, was all I had to do to be ordained into the sacred office of priest. Thank God, things are greatly changed today.

E.S.P.

There is a further Penge memory, pin-sharp in my mind, of a curious episode which happened in 1932 and which, nowadays, would come under the heading of E.S.P. I was sharply awakened in the small hours by a clearly defined picture of my sister, by that time a missionary teacher in India. She was leaning on a verandah and she was weeping in some acute distress. So sharp and vivid was this mental picture that I got out of bed and prayed earnestly for her until I felt she was to some degree comforted. I took careful note of the time and date as well as of the imagined verandah. (I had at no time before or since seen a photograph of the place where my sister was teaching or living.) In due course the answer came; my sister had indeed been in some considerable distress at the very time I had been awakened and had prayed. And she had, after a while, felt strangely comforted and at peace. And she was at the time on the verandah of the teacher's bungalow.

The nervous illness

As my third year in Penge went on my health began to deteriorate. I never had a serious headache in my life until I was ordained, nor did I ever have any trouble in getting to sleep. But now, in 1933 both the insomnia and the headaches were getting worse. I had a good deal of gastric pain and in general felt more and more nervous. Some time in the autumn I felt I could go on no longer. My doctor advised a long break. I felt it more honest and more sensible to resign the job altogether and try to sort my tensions out in my own time. It is true that I had no home to go to, and, in my nervous state, I did not fancy the hearty fervour of Father Trout's ménage. But I remembered a family whom I had met at Eastbourne during the seaside mission of a few years ago. They, with characteristic kindness, had kept in touch with me and had said that there was always a welcome for me in their house. They were as good as their word; and no words of gratitude from me can possibly express all the kindness and patience I received from this remarkable family. I think I was in love with the whole lot of them. The mother of the family is now dead, and so is the Nanny who had stayed on as a sort of companion housekeeper. The others are scattered in various parts of the world, but if these words come into their hands I would like to thank them publicly, so to speak, for the immeasurable debt I owe them for their unfailing love and friendship.

A few months before I left Penge I had changed my lodgings to Thicket Road, Anerley, a much more salubrious area than Penge. The establishment was run by two middle-aged ladies (short in stature but great in heart). They were relics of the Victorian age and had been left with nothing but the freehold possession of their house. This was still lighted only by gas, but with what now seems to me wholly admirable courage they shopped and cooked, washed and mended, and most generously fed a small number of paying guests.

It so happened that my sister would be home from India on furlough at Christmas-time, and so would her fiancé, Edwin Thornton Weekley, then a medical student at St. Thomas' Hospital. Thus we decided to spend Christmas, 1932, together at the house in Thicket Road, and I left for a time my beloved family at Eastbourne.

Hospital
After Christmas I was seized with violent abdominal pains and was forced to take to my bed. My usual G.P. said it was likely to be the aftermath of over-eating at the festival season, and prescribed some mild digestive nostrum. But the pains grew increasingly acute and my sister, bless her, rang another doctor for a second opinion. He diagnosed acute appendicitis, and within what seemed minutes an ambulance arrived to take me to Norwood Cottage Hospital, a couple of miles away. Once there they decided that I had general peritonitis and that I must be operated on as soon as possible. Frankly the internal agony was too great for me to think of anything else, but I would have consented to almost anything to get relief from the violent pain.

The operation was performed and I was so utterly exhausted that I could not speak nor even wink an eye. But I could still *hear* very acutely. (I have always remembered this when visiting patients who are seriously ill in hospital. They may appear unconscious, or even already dead, but in many

72

cases they can still *hear*. Hence the value of the quiet words of comfort or the simple prayer spoken in the patient's ear.)

In my case, utterly exhausted though I was, I heard the surgeon murmur, "He probably won't last the night, but make him as comfortable as you can."

A hint of the heavenly

I think that from earliest childhood I have always been aware of the eternal world. It often seemed to me that I lived in the here-and-now involuntarily, and perhaps a little impatiently. The innumerable clear and sharp experiences of childhood gave me hints and clues to beauty and reality which plainly transcended earthly life. I could not believe that this little life was my permanent home. The sweetness of music, the loveliness of nature and beauties of colour and form were at times intolerably sweet reminders of some permanent reality lying serenely beyond immediate perception. Doors opened momentarily only to shut again tantalisingly. One could only be aware of a fleeting glimpse of unutterable beauty. Now these inklings of eternity crystallised in a dream or vision so real and convincing that I can never forget it. I would not say that I felt then the presence of God as a person; I knew him rather as a kind of dimension. For I was a helpless human being resting entirely upon my Creator. God was as it were the sea of Being supporting me, infinitely compassionate and infinitely kind. Resting upon this support I fell asleep and had this startlingly vivid dream.

I was alone, depressed and miserable, trudging wearily down a dusty slope. Around me were the wrecks and refuse of human living. There were ruined houses, pools of stagnant water, cast-off shoes, rusty tin cans, worn-out motor tyres and rubbish of every kind. Suddenly, as I picked my way amid this dreary mess, I looked up. Not far away, on the other side of a little valley, was a vista of indescribable beauty. It seemed as though all the loveliness of mountain and stream, of field and forest, of cloud and sky were displayed with such intensity of beauty that I gasped for breath. The loveliest of scents were wafted across to me, the heart-piercing song of birds could be clearly heard, and the whole vision seemed to promise the answer to my deepest longings as much as the sight of water to a desperately thirsty man. I ran towards this glorious world. I knew intuitively that there lay the answer to all my questing, the satisfaction for all that I had most deeply desired. This shining fresh world was the welcoming frontier of my true and permanent home. I gathered my strength and ran down the dirty littered slope. I noticed that only a tiny stream separated me from all that glory and loveliness. Even as I ran, some little part of me noted with a lifting of the heart that Bunyan's "icy river" was, as I had long suspected, only a figment of his imagination. For not only was the stream a very narrow one, but as I approached I found that a shining white bridge had been built across it.

I ran towards that bridge, but even as I was about to set foot upon it, with my heart full of expectant joy, a figure in white appeared before me. He gave me the impression of supreme gentleness and absolute authority. He looked at me smiling and gently shook his head, at the same time pointing me back to the miserable slope down which I had so eagerly run. I have never known such bitter disappointment, and although I turned obediently enough I could not help bursting into tears. This passionate weeping must have awakened me, for the next thing that I remember was the figure of the night nurse bending over me and saying rather reproachfully, "What are you crying for? You've come through tonight – now you're going to live!" But my heart was too full of the vision for me to make any reply; what could I say to someone who had not seen what I had seen?

Years have passed since the night of that dream, and I can only say that it remains as true and clear to me today as it was then. Words are almost useless as a means to describe what I saw and felt, even though I have attempted to use them. I can only record my conviction that I saw reality that night, the bright, sparkling fringe of the world that is eternal. The vision has never faded.

Yet I woke in tears from this splendid unforgettable vision, and had no answer for the young nurse.

The hospital ward

There was much to be enjoyed, even in extreme weakness, of the general camaraderie of the ward. One man, all unknown to him, impressed me enormously. He was in because of an unpleasant boil on his neck. But he rarely stayed in bed. Quite unassumingly he helped in any way that he could and never shrank from assisting the nurses in the more messy tasks in the Sluice. Little by little, I was told of his own private life. He was a milkman, a strenuous and demanding task then as now, and he had had a few years of happily married life. Then his wife began to deteriorate mentally. She was in no sense violently insane, but became more and more retarded until she was mentally no more than a ten-year-old child.

The husband would have to wake up before 4 a.m., arrange for his wife's breakfast and lunch and then quietly, for safety's sake, lock her into their house until his duties stopped early in the afternoon. He would then spend hours reading to her or playing childish games.

Apparently someone in the ward had suggested to him that it would be better all round if she were put away in a place for the mentally retarded. He was a man who rarely spoke at all, but at this suggestion he is reported to have said, "Look, she's my wife and I married her for better or for worse. This may be the worse but it's my job to look after her. That's all there is to say."

I was too weak to hold much of a conversation with anyone, and I never exchanged more than a few words with this remarkable man. But his modest, almost self-effacing, ways shone like some beacon of sheer goodness and love. And yet, as far as I know, he was no churchgoer and certainly not a religious man in any conventional sense. This man, by the sheer pattern of his living, forced me to revise my ideas. Here was I, a saved Christian with all the right convictions but not possessing a millionth part of the practical outgoing love of this truly good man. I began to wonder whether the love and goodness of God works through very different channels from the ones that I had been taught to revere. This was the significant beginning of my suspicion of any group who thought they had a corner in the love and purposes of the Almighty.

At my supposed deathbed my father had murmured, "You won't get out of here under a hundred pounds, you know." He, poor man, meant that he was anxious at having to find such a sum himself, for he knew that I had almost no money. You can imagine my surprise when the time came for my discharge, and I had to see and thank the Matron, that she thought fifteen shillings would be an adequate charge. She knew, bless her, of the poverty of the assistant clergy, especially when out of work. But I insisted on making a donation of a few pounds to the hospital which had literally saved my life.

So I went back for a few days to the house of the two diminutive sisters in Anerley, and then down to Eastbourne to stay with the same affectionate and charming family. I picked up physically very rapidly indeed and after about three weeks was almost as good as new, in body. But I was still considerably muddled and tense over matters of religion, and shrank from re-entering into the life of a rather scared and shy curate.

The father of the Eastbourne family was himself a surgeon, and sent me to a famous Harley Street specialist for a thorough physical check. After a few routine checks, this man said, all in one sentence, "I wouldn't recommend you to go back to parish work, but I can do nothing for you, that will be five guineas please."

This was one of life's darkest moments and I can remember walking down Harley Street in a sort of daze of despair. Why had my life been saved by a hair's breadth if I was not to do the only work I had been trained for? I am not much of an enthusiast for plastering texts of scripture about the place, but in all honesty I must say that I was, in this bleak moment of despondency, greatly cheered by a huge illuminated text displayed in the window of the Scripture Union's shop in Wigmore Street. "The Lord . . . He it is that doth go before thee," it read and those words brought me great comfort. There must *be* a plan and purpose, although I could not see it at the moment.

Leonard Browne

Thus I returned once more to Eastbourne, puzzled and temporarily defeated, but certainly not in despair. This time the father of the family, who was not only a brilliant surgeon but a man of very considerable insight, decided that my trouble must be psychological and arranged for me to see the best psychiatrist I have ever met. He was Leonard Browne, and he then had rooms in Wimpole Street. His modest commonsense manner did not immediately inform me that here was an outstanding man of quite exceptional gifts. He was a personal friend of Jung and one of the founders of the Tavistock Clinic, and when I later came to look him up in *Who's Who* I was dazzled at the prizes and distinctions he had won. He is, alas, now dead, but I had the pleasure of meeting him in retirement at Grange-in-Borrowdale a year or two before he died.

Leonard Browne set me on my feet in a very short time, although the treatment lasted several weeks. I did not know it at the time, but he was a convinced Christian. Nevertheless he gently insisted that my problems and tensions were not really religious – it was simply that I had been putting them into a religious form. Following the Jung technique I lay on a couch, and later sat in a chair, and by answering a series of gentle but probing questions came to see for myself that the seeds of my present distress were sown in early childhood. What I was now projecting on to "God" was no more than the unconscious shadow of the demanding perfectionist father of my earliest days. The more I recollected the more strongly I could see that I was setting myself an impossible standard reinforced by religious sanctions.

I began to recover quite quickly as the tensions began to be seen for what they were. I did not yet feel that I could return to the grind of parochial life, but I could not live with the Eastbourne family for ever. I spent a few weeks with an aunt at East Sheen and wrote a number of children's stories (now mercifully all out of print) to cover Dr. Browne's very modest fees.

The Pathfinder Press

Then quite out of the blue, an old Cambridge friend, Roger de Pemberton, invited me to be editorial secretary of the Pathfinder Press. As the office of this now defunct press was in London, I moved back again to Anerley to stay yet once more with the stout-hearted if diminutive "aunties". I know I earned very little money but I could just manage to pay for board and lodging and for daily commuting to north London. The main work was to produce a quarterly magazine called the *Pathfinder* (a magazine devoted to general as well as Christian subjects), to publish from time to time what we called *Pathfinder Pamphlets*, and naturally to answer the quite considerable correspondence. My staff was one shorthand typist and a good-natured hard-working office girl. All three of us worked pretty strenuously, and once a quarter almost to the point of physical exhaustion. All the thousands of magazines (I have forgotten the total but it was quite considerable) had to be packed and stamped by hand and then carried, batch by batch, to the local post office.

That period of something over a year gave me much useful experience in the art of editing, and of the problems of typesetting. I also spent quite a lot of my time searching photographic agencies for suitable pictures to illustrate our articles and to arrange the payment of a reasonable fee. One way and another I learnt quite a lot about the difficult art of producing a magazine.

The magazine was not a great success financially, and before long I had to accept a cut in an already meagre salary. Once more, as in my early Cambridge days, life had to be lived on a shoestring. In addition, since we could not afford to pay contributors, I found myself writing nearly all the articles myself, under different names, *and* drawing for line and half-tone blocks. Despite this however, I did receive two free benefits. One was to help run a Christian house party for young people, in Swanage. The other was to help staff a similar house party, though this time a skiing holiday, at St. Anton in Austria. The idea of these was to get together some fifty or sixty young men and women, mostly in their early twenties, and to propose and discuss the Christian faith in informal surroundings. Naturally a lot of fun was enjoyed in between the serious sessions, and I like to think some useful work was done both at Swanage and at St. Anton.

6

St. Margaret's, Lee, Marriage and Wartime
1936–1941

I can remember that I was one of the curates at St. Margaret's just before the Second World War and my contemporaries were Alan Cooper and Paul Biddlecombe. We worked under that extraordinary man Canon F. H. Gillingham, and we learnt a great deal from him. Above all he taught us how to conduct a service properly. In fact he was a bit of a perfectionist, and in our early days with him he made us learn the church lessons by heart to make sure they were always meaningfully read. He also taught us how to use pauses and changes of pace in the conduct of any service. This minute attention to detail meant that no one of any sensitivity could attend any service at St. Margaret's and remain completely unmoved. Of course we complained among ourselves and I felt that "Gilly" was treating us like slaves; perhaps he was, but I have remembered the polished result for all these forty years.

Gilly
In 1936 I received a telephone call from a Canon Gillingham inviting me to be his curate. He was then rector of St. Margaret's, Lee (adjoining Blackheath in south-east London) and was expecting to move to All Souls, Langham Place, next door to Broadcasting House in London. This seemed to me to be too good an opportunity to miss, and in a few days I went down to see the good canon in his rectory. By this time it was by no means sure that he would be offered the living of All Soul's, Langham Place, but would I, he asked, be prepared to

help him in the parish of St. Margaret's, Lee? I liked Gilly (as everyone called him) at first sight and I accepted with some alacrity.

By the time I joined his staff evensong had had to be duplicated; one service was at 5.45 p.m. and the other at 7 p.m. A different choir, and indeed a different organist, were used at these two evensongs, and therefore, in theory at least, the same sermon could be preached twice. Nevertheless, each of us found it a considerable effort to take these two consecutive services, after having already conducted two or three services that day, and still maintain the freshness of expression on which Gilly, quite rightly, insisted. We also learnt from him how to conduct a funeral sympathetically but never mawkishly, and how to take the service of holy matrimony with love but without sentimentality. He was very good in his personal dealings with people, and he was immensely popular. His preaching was for the most part excellent, and he certainly knew how to put it across.

I knew that Gilly was a favourite after-dinner speaker, though I never heard him myself. I also knew that he had a fantastic memory and that one of his party pieces was to recite the whole of Dicken's *Christmas Carol* by heart. But it took me a few weeks to discover that his brilliantly delivered sermons were not his original work at all. They were the impeccably memorised sermons of others, among whom I remember James Reid and George Morrison. I was horrified to discover that some of these sermons were being printed in the parish magazine as sermons "preached by Canon F. H. Gillingham". This was too much for me. I showed him a book by the Presbyterian minister James Reid in which a certain chapter had been reproduced word for word in the parish magazine as Gilly's own sermon. I don't think he ever stopped cribbing other people's sermons, but at least I persuaded him to make suitable acknowledgements to the original writer in the parish magazine.

Blackheath

I lived at the rectory for nearly a year and saw pretty clearly both the great gifts and the petty weaknesses of a fascinating

81

man. But it fairly soon dawned on me that it was not really a good thing to live in the same house as one's employer, and I therefore took a bed-sitter in a well-run guest house in Blackheath. It was in this house that I met my wife.

This guest house provided accommodation for about twenty people, mostly in their late teens or early twenties, and we were very happy together. Our occupations were varied: a young manager of a shipping firm, a radio salesman, a schoolmistress, an army major, a salesgirl and a worker for the G.P.O. film unit. And particularly there were two teachers of dancing from the Blackheath Conservatoire, and their pianist. I say particularly because one of the dancing teachers was before long to become my wife. Also in the house, which was really two adjoining houses made into one, were a Russian, a Dutchman and a Dane. What they did we never discovered. We lived singularly innocent lives. All of us were hard-working in our respective spheres and none of us had much money to spare. We were well fed and full of high spirits. But whereas I suppose in a similar situation today we should all be hopping in and out of one another's beds, very little of that sort of thing ever happened. We were not yet living in a permissive age.

Attitudes to women

Apart from the grace of God, which can operate in all sorts of unexpected ways, I can see certain definite traits in my own character which kept me relatively innocent, if not ignorant, as I began seriously to consider marriage.

First, I had an innate respect for women. No doubt this was much influenced by my admiration and love for my mother, and probably by my father's devotion to her especially in the latter years of her illness. I regarded all women as essentially good and it honestly took me years to discover that there are nasty, greedy, self-centred and unscrupulous women.

Second, although I always seem to have had a lot of girl-friends, and in general got on well with women, I had not the faintest idea that I could be personally attractive to them. The idea did not dawn upon me until I was nearly in my fifties.

But very probably this utter lack of knowledge of any attractiveness of my own saved me from any serious trouble.

Third, I had an instinctive recoil from any female who appeared to be making advances towards me. I was, and indeed am, a fairly simple character and the whole idea of a woman pursuing a man struck me as unnatural and repulsive.

Fourth, when in the presence of women I talked and joked and laughed with them without regarding them as sexual beings at all. I enjoy the company of a pretty girl or a beautiful woman as much as the next man, but I am never tempted mentally to undress them. It simply does not enter my head.

Fifth, and again probably because of my love for my sick and tired mother, I have always felt strongly protective towards the other sex. Life has taught me that a good many women are much stronger than I am, some even physically, but the attitude persists. I think women know this by some sort of instinct, and I think they also know that I would never do anything against their will.

All these things sound as though I behaved very well towards women and had nothing more to learn. In fact this was far from being the case. I had in my younger days very strong sexual desires, which seemed to me inherently sinful. It was chiefly through the help of Leonard Browne that I learnt to join love and sex together and to get them to work in the same direction. And that was not learnt in five minutes.

Vera

Vera Jones had been living in the local Y.W.C.A., but had left it in disgust because all lights were turned off at a ridiculously early hour; usually when after a hard day's work she was enjoying a hot bath. The chances of our meeting in the ordinary way were improbable in the highest degree. I knew nothing of the world of dancing. I tried to understand ballet from a book Vera lent me but I don't feel the same instinctive appreciation for this form of art that I do for music and painting. I have tried to analyse this and I think it is because the personality of the artist obtrudes itself. That is also why I dislike singing. In instrumental music (especially orchestral) and in painting it is possible to be in direct touch with the artist's interpretation of beauty without being bothered by the artist himself. Of course if you admire art for the artist's sake it is different, but I don't; I regard the artist as simply the medium through which beauty is born into the world. Therefore he is, in his functioning, quite unimportant. I don't see how he can do this in ballet, nor, on a casual impression, do I feel that people who are keen on ballet care about this. I did my very best to appreciate ballet because I knew it meant so much to Vera and she is also good at it.

Vera, brought up in Yorkshire in a vaguely congregational atmosphere, knew little of the Church of England and its attempts to bring Christianity into the life of the late 1930s. But fate, coincidence, or the hand of Providence led us to live in the same house and to get to know each other. It was not only her beauty and charm, but her utter reliability and integrity which overwhelmed me. We had both had some unhappy experience in matters of the heart before and it was not without some misgivings (we called them Mrs. Givings) on both sides that she finally agreed to marry me. I still don't know why she married me; she could not have foreseen any of my successful future as a writer, and was committing herself to be the wife of a curate earning some seven pounds a week. All I can say is that she was, and is, a most remarkable woman.

As for me I did so want to have a nice home. I couldn't expect Vera (with her independent streak) to want a home as much as I did, but I did long for a peaceful and comfortable centre from which to work and to which I could return. I felt sure it would make a lot of difference to me and I was prepared to give a lot to make the dream come true. With Vera's dancing I knew that I was asking for a sacrifice but writing to her I said, "I am hoping one day that it will mean more than anything else to you to help make this home. I realise that it will mean the heavier end of the burden for you but I will do my share I promise you."

How my attitude had changed. At one time I honestly thought that the girl who married me would be damned lucky. Now I was trying to see things quite differently. I wrote instead to Vera, "I think there will come a day when I become someone worthwhile but I'm afraid I get pretty discouraged. It isn't really like me to be so moody and irritable. Still if you love me, it'll have to be 'take me as I am', I'll do my best to make you happy."

My letters to her show something of how I loved her:

Yes, sweetheart, there are some drifting icebergs, but I love you. Darling, don't be frightened at all, will you? Your Jack's best side is his "protective" one. You haven't seen much of it yet because you're so competent, but here I am, to lean on if you need me.

God bless you, dear, and keep you close to Himself whatever you may be doing. I do thank Him for the joy that is beginning to creep back into life.

The memory of you and your dearness and sweetness is still with me. How I hope this is all going to turn to real deep happiness for us both. Let us go on praying that we may see the right way quite clearly.

I know a little of the blackness of nervous depression but I am sure you don't want to hear any more of my psychological troubles but the last two days have been very grim indeed. I think the thought of your disappointment if I failed to battle through helped me a lot.

I could almost say that the latter stages of my courtship took place "on Ilkla moor ba't'at". Certainly I proposed and was accepted in a delightful church in a Yorkshire dale. My fiancée's parents were then living at Guiseley, a few miles outside Bradford, and we had a glorious holiday in that magnificent scenery.

Marriage

We duly returned to Blackheath and fixed our wedding day for 19th April (Primrose day) in 1939. We were given many presents and in spite of Gilly's printed slip to the effect that presents to me were not to exceed two and sixpence the parish gave us a splendid radiogram. The wedding was conducted by Canon F. H. Gillingham in St. Margaret's, Lee.

There are those who set great store by the promises made in church "before God and this congregation". But in the happy marriage which goes on growing stronger and deeper as the years pass, no reference is ever made to those promises. I do not say that the promises are valueless, but I do say that you cannot make a marriage by external laws, and that something has gone seriously wrong with the marriage if the partners of it have to remind each other of the promises made years before.

Those who are happily married know very well that their union is in fact indissoluble. There is a personal union of love, shared interests and common experience, so that divorce becomes not only unthinkable but appears like the tearing apart of the living person.

We had a most enjoyable reception and were lent a brand new small car for our honeymoon. We had high hopes of exploring the beauties of Sussex in spring, but we were hardly settled in our rooms in Alfriston when I went down with influenza. It is a melancholy distinction, but I have sometimes thought I must be the only man who went down with 'flu on his honeymoon. The best we could do was for Vera to tour the country during the day and tell me of her travels in the evening.

Our first home was a top flat in a charming house in Blackheath, and since our tastes were simple, and thanks to the generous wedding gifts from relations, friends and individual parishioners we did not feel we were living in penury. For the time being Vera continued her work as before, the only difference for me was that our responsibilities as curates had been swapped around somewhat and I found myself primarily in charge of a small church called Boone's Chapel, so-called from the man who built both the chapel and the surrounding almshouses. I well remember making deaf-aids and fitting them to several pews. Once again maximum ingenuity had to be used for I had to pay for such a luxury out of my own pocket.

War

It hardly needs saying here that no one took Chamberlain's reassurance of "peace in our time" very seriously, though we thought it gave us a breathing space in which to take certain precautions. In early 1939 our great fear was the use of poison gas, and I can remember trying, with the assistance of willing helpers, to make the living quarters of the almshouse inhabitants as gas-proof as possible. In the light of future events this seems ludicrous but our hard work was serious enough.

As many will remember, the declaration of war came on a sunny Sunday in September 1939. The first sirens blew their eerie warning and I was sharply told to "take cover" by a passing air-raid warden on a bicycle. I remember this because I was in fact putting the finishing touches to one of my gas-proof almshouses, before taking the morning service. Well, the "all clear" sounded soon afterwards and no further raids, real or imaginary, happened for nearly a year. It was the period called by the Americans the Phoney War.

The Church of the Good Shepherd

But the declaration of war made quite a difference to me. There was a church about a mile from St. Margaret's called the Church of the Good Shepherd. The vicar of this church, who had been a chaplain in the First World War and was on the reserve list, left his post almost as soon as war was declared and re-joined the army. Gilly therefore decided that I should become priest-in-charge of the Church of the Good Shepherd as well as helping in the general work of St. Margaret's. These new duties included a week's stint per month at conducting all the funerals that took place in the borough of Lewisham. Quite often this meant forty or fifty funerals in a single week and led me to spend many a day at the Hither Green cemetery, complete with sandwiches and vacuum flask. For the next few months I did all this without a halfpenny of extra salary and naturally all the funeral fees went, as far as I could see, into Gilly's pocket. The appointment to the living of the Good Shepherd, Lee, was a prerogative of the rector of St. Margaret's, namely the same Gilly. The previous vicar, the Reverend Leslie Hills, had in early 1940 resigned the benefice but it was not until June of that year that I became officially vicar of the Good Shepherd, Lee.

The vicarage was vast and Victorian and we decided that we could afford neither to heat nor furnish it, even though my income had now reached nearly £500. We therefore rented a small semi-detached house, and as things turned out this was a very wise move. For when the blitz started in earnest, there was in the vicarage temporary accommodation for the bombed-out. Later when the church itself was destroyed by fire and the parish hall converted into a church, the same vicarage was used for Sunday School, youth club, mothers' union and indeed for all parochial meetings.

From the beginning we found ourselves very happy at the Church of the Good Shepherd. The congregations were never large, though they grew. We had an excellent organist and choirmaster, "Pop" Smith, and a choir good by any standard. I had occasional help from two splendid retired priests, the Reverend W. P. Parker and the Reverend L. Steele. As the war went on Bill Parker died, but many is the night that we sat under the kitchen table with Louis and Nan Steele. I never saw them frightened or in any way dismayed by many weeks of night bombing and the general stress of daily living.

Air raids

Our first real experience of the war was the sudden start of the historic Battle of Britain. For over a year we had grown accustomed to the balloon barrage, a matter of many thousand captive hydrogen-filled balloons floating over London and its surroundings. The idea was that the steel cables which confined this massive pattern would prevent the practice of dive-bombing. But we had almost never seen an aeroplane. Suddenly on that gloriously sunny September day there appeared what seemed to be hundreds of German bombers intent on the destruction of London.

I, as it happened, had just finished conducting a funeral and was on my way home on my bicycle. It seems ridiculous now, but I put my head down and pedalled furiously to get home. I suppose the bombers were travelling at around 250 miles an hour and my cycling speed was scarcely a tenth of that and a few seconds could hardly have mattered. Yet I did reach home just as the first bomb was dropped on my parish. No one was hurt and, since it was only a small bomb, the material damage was only slight.

My wife and I were fascinated as we watched our own Hurricanes and Spitfires, outnumbered by at least twenty to one, weaving in and out of the attacking force and shooting down several of the enemy. The roaring drone of aeroplane engines was tremendous and above it the constant crackle of cannon fire. Now and again came the sickening rising scream of an aeroplane diving to earth out of control, to be followed by a "crump" and blazing pillar of fire. At times the air seemed to be full of parachutes as Germans, and a few of our own pilots, dropped out of their stricken planes. It was an unforgettable sight and left me with a lasting impression of the superhuman courage of our young pilots who came in again and again to destroy, or at least reduce the force which was hell-bent on destroying our capital city.

As we all know, it was not long before our fighters were exacting such a toll on the Luftwaffe that daytime bombing en masse ceased. The switch was made to night bombing, and, like many others, we endured many months of night blitz. The almost continual roar of anti-aircraft guns, the droning of planes and, for us in the suburbs, the occasional dropping of high explosive or incendiary bombs in our areas continued for many weeks. It was not safe to be in the street because of the hail of shrapnel-splinters from anti-aircraft shells. Slates and tiles were broken every night. I have no wish to disparage the wearisome efforts of the gunners but, until the end of the war, I never saw any shell hit any aircraft. It was said that the barrage was maintained to keep up our morale – to make us feel that we were being protected – but it was a noisy price to pay for what appeared to be highly problematical protection.

In October 1941, during one of the fiercest raids directed against London docks, a stray German plane set fire to our church. Incendiary bombs lodged between the roof proper and the barrel roof inside. Within seconds the place was fiercely ablaze. All fire-fighting equipment had been sent to save our precious food supplies at the docks, and we were helpless, with our little standard stirrup-pumps, to do anything to check the fire. I can remember being restrained from dashing into the church to save some of its few valuables, and indeed it would have been impossible. And I can remember begging the crowd of several hundreds who had collected to go home. German planes were roaring overhead and we, sharply illuminated by the monstrous blaze, were a sitting target for any bomb-happy German pilot. Eventually people did go home, and by next morning the church, which was largely made of wood, was a smoking ruin. Nevertheless at first light we had put up a defiant notice, "We carry on."

The parish hall church

By some extraordinary chance, or providence, the parish hall, a corrugated iron structure less than six feet from the church itself, was scorched but otherwise undamaged. Within a week my wife and I, ably assisted by my verger, a Mr. Harrott who had been a skilled wheelwright, and of course many others, had converted that dismal shack into a place fit for worship. A local church which had also been almost completely destroyed offered us an altar cross and candlesticks, and sufficient undamaged pews for us to seat nearly two hundred. We were also given a carpet, prayer books and hymn books. Our own altar cross, which had been dug out of the wreckage, was cleaned and re-polished and became our processional cross. We received scores of hours of voluntary work in matters of painting, re-wiring and replacing cracked windows. The lectern and pulpit were made largely of hardboard but no one would have noticed that, so skilfully did Mr. Harrott and his helpers use the very small stock of wood which we could find. The same fine man and skilled craftsman made me a plain cross of oak rescued from the pile of charred wreckage, and it stands on my desk to this day.

It would be impossible to remember all the good friends who offered help, but a gesture which was to remain in my mind was the offer of the use of their church made by our local congregational brethren. They even offered to change the times of their own services to suit our convenience. The offer was deeply appreciated, but we had no need to accept it. In an incredibly short space of time we had our own church again, cosy and easy to black-out, and it was soon licensed by the bishop for all services, including holy matrimony.

Air-raid casualties

It was not long after the destruction of the church that our first really heavy bomb fell. It made at least a dozen houses uninhabitable, and we were able to give the occupants temporary shelter in the vicarage. Many of us had at that time no real shelter. Anderson shelters, which were little steel cabins fixed partly underground and which owners were expected to erect themselves, were available free to those whose income was under five pounds a week (if memory serves me). The rest of us were, I suppose, considered to have enough money to have at least one room, or cellar, properly strengthened. We, like many others, could not afford this and used to huddle under the staircase – this having been proved by experience to be comparatively the safest place if a house were destroyed.

A great deal of damage was done to property during the months of night bombing but there were surprisingly few casualties. I was still doing a weekly turn at conducting funerals, but usually very few of those deaths were due to enemy action. There was, however, one terrible exception which remains fixed in my mind. In daylight a German fighter dived under the balloon barrage, dropped a few small bombs and then deliberately opened machine-gun fire on a crowd of young children in the playground of Catford School. If my memory serves me, something like thirty-nine children were killed, and they were buried in a mass grave at Hither Green cemetery, the service being conducted by the Bishop of Southwark. Four thousand attended the service and a huge crowd followed the cortège in utter silence. We were more or less prepared to accept the fact that the Germans were determined to destroy our food supplies and, by general destruction of property, to break our spirit. We were even prepared to accept the fact that bomb aiming was inaccurate and that quite often the wrong targets were hit, but this could have been no mistake; the visibility was excellent. It was the first time we had irrefutable evidence of what was called in the First World War "German frightfulness". The crowd walked silently in a cold passion of anger. The general feeling was not a lust for revenge but a renewed determination that Nazism must be utterly destroyed.

Although, as I have said, the cables of the barrage balloons were designed to prevent low-level attacks by aircraft they were not always effective, as shown by the above tragic and evil incident.

One foggy night, when one might have expected even the most intrepid night fighters to have stayed at their air bases, two aircraft zoomed down almost to rooftop height at incredible speed, firing at each other in the dark. One of the bullets missed me by a hand's breadth and exploded on the pavement a few feet in front of me. I was unhurt, and I still have the bullet. The wires of the balloon barrage *could* be evaded, and this was shown again and again by the indomitable fighters who lay in wait on the outskirts of London to shoot down the pilotless V.1s.

Meanwhile, towards the end of the war we enjoyed comparative peace. Table shelters, simple rugged cages with extremely strong steel tops and corner girders, were available to us all, although they remained little used until the flying bombs arrived. Shelters for the general public had been excavated on various sites, and brick blast shelters as well as emergency water tanks appeared in the streets. It fairly soon became plain, however, that the most numerous casualties occurred *in* shelters. It was simply because fifty or a hundred people collected together were liable to be killed one and all by the freakish effect of blast if a large bomb fell nearby. Thus there was a general policy of dispersement and we were asked, as in other churches, to avoid the collecting of many people together as far as we could. The period of conducting short services in shelters was discontinued fairly early, and I and my fellow clergy and ministers would do our best to take religious services in people's homes. I can still remember that the burden of my short addresses on these occasions rested on the assurance of St. Paul, "*in* all these things we are more than conquerors". The point, which was aimed at me as much as at my scattered flock, was that the early Church was in danger (just as we were in danger) but they were assured that it is actually *in* such perils that they were "more than conquerors".

7

Letters to Young Churches
1941–1947

I began the work of translation as long ago as 1941, and the work was undertaken primarily for the benefit of my youth club, and members of my congregation, in a much bombed parish in south-east London. I had almost no tools to work with apart from my own Greek Testament and no friends who could help me in this particular field. I felt that since much of the New Testament was written to Christians in danger, it should be particularly appropriate for us who, for many months, lived in a different, but no less real danger. I began with the epistles, since most of my Christian members had at least a nodding acquaintance with the gospels, but regarded the epistles as obscure and difficult and therefore largely unread. In those days of danger and emergency I was not over-concerned with minute accuracy; I wanted above all to convey the vitality and radiant faith as well as the courage of the early Church.

A church in wartime

It is impossible for me to exaggerate the magnificent spirit shown without exception by these south-east Londoners. Of course we were all frightened from time to time, but I never saw any kind of despair. We all lost window-glass quite early in the war. It was replaced by the flimsiest of roofing felt. Yet I never saw or heard of any thief breaking and entering nor did I know of any looting from damaged shops. The general feeling was unbelievably friendly, anybody being ready at any time to help anybody else.

We enjoyed the free use of a splendid sports ground,

belonging to a firm whose staff had been evacuated from London, on the sole condition that we kept the grass cut. Many of us, young and old, enjoyed this amenity and there was never a lack of volunteers to work the massive ancient lawnmower.

It would be impossible for me to mention by name the enormous number of men and women, young and old, who helped to maintain morale and to pack our little church Sunday by Sunday. But I must mention my lady worker, Sister Marjorie Green, who was almost as good as a curate in the ministry, and better than many curates in her quiet, busy faithfulness. She died, alas, soon after the war, and I am still ashamed of the fact that I did not make time in an admittedly busy schedule to visit her as she lay dying in hospital.

Just before the unexpected attack of Hitler's first secret weapon, the V.1 or flying bomb, we had a sudden sharp attack of incendiary bombs. It has its funny side, for we were all attending a meeting of fire-watchers. We had just been told that if there were a fire we were not to rush off and put it out but to report it (in triplicate) to the nearest warden's post and then wait for instructions. These new regulations were to come into force within the next few days, but as soon as these words were pronounced the sirens began to wail. We left hurriedly and before many of us had reached our houses quite the most severe load of incendiaries fell on our parish. Many, of course, blazed away in gardens looking like garish fireworks, but it was obvious that many homes had been struck. My wife, with customary commonsense, suggested that we might inspect our house first. It was just as well that we did, for one of these bombs had struck our house and was blazing away in the ceiling of my study. Despite all our precious training in the use of the stirrup-pump, we spilled a great deal of water extinguishing this fire before we went out to join the other householders in the road. I think there were over forty fires in our road and we were proud of the fact that we put out all but two by use of our stirrup-pumps. The others were dealt with by what was then the auxiliary fire service.

Frankly I don't remember the first V.1, but we soon got sickeningly familiar with the peculiar phut-phut of its engine, the seconds of silence, and then the inevitable crump of a thousand pounds of high explosive hitting a building, or the ground, and the inevitable pall of dust. As time went on we grew faintly contemptuous of this terror weapon. Experience had shown that if you had a good solid brick wall behind which to shelter you were not likely to be seriously hurt. Nevertheless, although casualties in general were surprisingly low, the damage to buildings, houses, roads, water and gas mains, bridges and railway lines was considerable.

Anyone who had lived through the experience of being bombed for many months has his own stock of bomb stories. Naturally I have plenty, some tragic, some funny to the point of farce, but I don't propose to bore my readers with my own stories. I will, however, tell of two happenings, one of which was, I think providential, and the other, which could have been tragic but turned out to have its comic side.

Two bomb stories

During one of the periods of night bombing my wife and I, instead of following our usual practice of walking through two back gardens to join the courageous elderly couple I have already mentioned to shelter under their kitchen table, decided to walk round on the pavement and post a letter at the corner pillar-box. We both knew that the latest collection had been taken, but without hesitation decided to post the letter that night. Within a few seconds of our doing so there came the unmistakable whistling whine of a stick of bombs. The pattern was plainly moving in our direction so we flung ourselves down on the pavement, my wife asking me at what angle one should wear the tin hat in a prone position. Before I had time to answer we both received a violent thump on the chin as the pavement seemingly rose up to smite us. At the same time came the devastating roar of an exploding bomb – number nine of the stick according to our reckoning. We did not know of course whether this was the last and lay still for a minute or two. Then we got up, joined our friends, and were informed that a crater, some twenty feet across and seven deep, had appeared in the back garden, in the very path we would normally have taken. We were very thankful that we both felt it right to post a letter that night. And everyone was delighted when, a few months later, the most splendid vegetable marrows were grown at the bottom of the crater, in soil which had probably been undisturbed for many centuries and was in a rather peculiar sense virgin.

The other incident happened while I was conducting a funeral at Hither Green cemetery. A V.1 with its unmistakable noise was apparently heading straight for us and within seconds the engine cut out. "Down everybody!" I shouted, and there we lay flat on the ground on the clay around the graveside. Out of the corner of my eye I saw the flying bomb coming straight at us – it could not have been more than seventy yards away and would plunge any second. My chief thought was to wonder at the high polish given to the nose of the lethal little craft. "Why bother to polish it?" I could not help thinking. Then it crashed and the ground all around us shook as if by an earthquake. Then followed a frantic scream as of many missiles in flight. I therefore waited a few more seconds before asking everyone to stand in their places as before, while I continued the burial service. The bomb had, we soon discovered, fallen into an allotment some fifty yards away and had completely removed a crop of full-grown cabbages. It was their bullet-heads, travelling at what must surely be a record speed for cabbages, which had made those unnerving screams. I still find myself amazed that both the mourners and I went through that experience completely unshaken, and that our comments were thankful but brief.

Flying bombs

At the time of the fiercest flying-bomb attacks I thought it wise to discontinue at least our Sunday evening services in the little church. The whole building, which was usually crammed with nearly 200 people, was as flimsy as a house of cards, and would collapse instantly if there were the merest whiff of blast. But my congregation would have none of this. "Where," they asked me, "could we better die, if we have to die, than in the house of God?" This spirit was unanswerable and the evening services were continued. I did stipulate that

97

an electric bell should be placed in the church, and that this should be operated by one of the wardens in the nearby post if one of the V.1s should be seen diving directly at the church. The button was never pressed, but if one of these noisy instruments of death buzzed its way very near at hand it was not unusual to see people crouch down (not in fear but with prudence) in their pews and sometimes I saw old ladies cover their heads with scarves or mackintoshes.

But these flying bombs were now flying a little above rooftop height, and the noise was considerable. They were able to do this because, by some near-miracle of organisation, London's roof of barrage balloons had been moved outwards some twenty miles into the surrounding countryside. This was accomplished almost overnight without fuss and indeed without official announcement that I can remember. The theory was that if some of these pilotless planes could be tripped by cable in the open country and explode there many lives would be saved. The theory worked, at least up to a point, and we ourselves, while having a few days break at Tonbridge in Kent, saw a number of these machines hit a cable, possibly shearing a wing, lose stability and plunge into the open fields. We also saw some feats of almost incredible bravery on the part of R.A.F. pilots. They would wait high above the V.1s and, identifying them at night by the flame of their exhausts, would power-dive down at I suppose speeds of some 400 m.p.h. and attack them with cannon-fire. Men were stationed outside the barrage to fire red warning rockets if a pilot seemed liable to enter the danger zone. But these immensely courageous young pilots, once on the trail of their quarry, were not easily deterred. They just pressed on regardless and we saw many of the terror weapons destroyed. Of course what they aimed to do was to shoot off the wings of the "plane" and force it to dive. But sometimes they hit the warhead itself and there was a tremendous mid-air explosion. By sheer speed and skill many, though not alas all, escaped to return to the attack.

Before many months passed Hitler's second secret weapon, the V.2, had begun to descend on London. There was, at the time, no defence of any kind against these weapons, and since they travelled at a speed faster than sound, there was no warning noise of their coming. To some people this made these horrors less terrifying since you were spared the nerve-fraying wait between the noise and the actual explosion. To me they were very frightening indeed since there was no chance of taking shelter. I was not, and am not, afraid to die, but the thought of being blinded or maimed, or both, without warning made me more afraid than at any other time during the war. I was once just getting out of a train at London Bridge when a V.2 fell in the forecourt of that terminus. The tremendous explosion came first, closely followed by a brutal wave of blast which flung me back into the compartment. And then, fractionally later came the noise of the bomb's passage sounding like a hundred express trains at once. Fortunately for me this was my closest acquaintance with any of these supersonic horrors, but they haunted my imagination day and night. We could not help hearing the noise of their explosions, nor avoid seeing the appalling devastation that they brought.

The King's Own
  Some of my happiest memories of this period are connected with the youth club. This was a flourishing group of young people known as the King's Own which met at the vicarage on weekdays, and after evensong on Sunday evenings, for all sorts of activities from ballroom dancing to making lamp-shades. At the close of these activities I used to read some verses of Paul's epistles. After all, I thought to myself, much of this was written by one Christian in difficulty to other Christians in difficulty, and surely these young people will find them appropriate to their situation. But I was met by polite but complete lack of comprehension. These youngsters, who were by no means unintelligent, simply did not understand Bible language. All my old passion for making truth comprehensible, and all my desire to do a bit of real translation, urged me to put some relevant New Testament truths into language which these young people could understand. This I did and was rewarded beyond my expectations as they realised for the first time, not merely that the epistles of Paul really could

make sense, but that the inspired words were extremely relevant to life as they knew it.

It was out of these Sunday evening meetings that *Letters to Young Churches* was born. I sent a copy of my new translation of Colossians to C. S. Lewis, whose work I had been admiring for the last few years. His reply was short and encouraging.

Aug. 3rd 1943   Magdalen College, Oxford

Dear Mr. Phillips, Thank you a hundred times. I thought I knew *Colossians* pretty well but your paraphrase made it far more significant – it was like seeing a familiar picture after it's been cleaned. The third paragraph on p.4 and the first on p.5 helped me particularly. The only thing I thought unfortunate is "Life from nothing began with Him" at the bottom of p.3. This might mean that Christ was created *ex nihilo*, instead of begotten. I hope very much you will carry on your plan of doing all the epistles. Of course you'll be opposed tooth and nail by all the "cultured" asses who say you're only spoiling "the beauty" of A.V. – all the people who objected to *Green Pastures* and *Man Born to be King* and who are always waffling about reverence. But we must kill that! I hope you'll add a little plain preface – all popular theology, no gas about St. Paul's "personality" or the wild flowers of Palestine – and a really full analytical index. The index by itself will blow to bits all the modern exaggerations of the difference between Pauline and Johannine theology. Heartiest good wishes, yours sincerely C. S. Lewis

P.S. Thank you for all your kind references to my own works.

Invitation to Redhill

In the latter part of 1944, the Bishop of Southwark offered me the living of St. John's, Redhill, about twenty miles away in Surrey. (The war was almost over by now, and the bishop thought those who had endured a London parish throughout the blitz should be moved to the country.) I must confess that on visiting the parish I was so appalled at the vastness of the task that I almost at once refused. However, the bishop (Dr.

B. F. Simpson) pressed me to reconsider, and eventually I agreed to go on condition that I could have the help of an assistant curate.

A farewell letter

It was to me a heart-rending decision. I reprint here an extract from one of the last letters I wrote for the parish magazine of the Good Shepherd, Lee. I wrote it to and for some of the finest people I have ever met.

Meanwhile I, for one, salute you civilians! I salute you as you go up to work by the same train, bombs or no bombs. I salute you housewives who shop and plan your rations and do your housework, bombs or no bombs. I salute all that army of men and women who come forward to help the moment an incident has occurred. I salute your cheerfulness and courage. They have not been the least of the forces which have brought us, by God's help, through five long years to the prospect of victory.

Beginnings at Redhill

We arrived in Redhill in January, 1945, a few days before my institution and induction on the Feast of the Epiphany, January 6th. It was bitterly cold and snow lay thick upon the ground. The vicarage was a pleasant modern one, even equipped with central heating, but coke was then rationed and we could not use the main boiler even if we had been able to afford it. Until our furniture arrived we crouched by a single-bar electric fire. We had two wooden "parish" chairs, and I think we must have slept on the floor. Sometimes, when ice and snow permitted, we would drive round our parish-to-be in the secondhand Austin 7 which was our farewell present from the Church of the Good Shepherd. We were enchanted by the beauties of the surrounding countryside, but appalled at the size of the task awaiting me.

I have no wish to denigrate the good people of St. John's, Redhill, and indeed in the ten years we stayed there we made a number of friends. But, apart from the faithful few, it is

101

difficult to imagine a parish more different from the one in which we spent the war years. For one thing it was inexorably divided into three strata: one was the residue of the old pastoral life and its descendants and they lived in a distinct part of the parish called Meadvale. Then, in the part of the parish which ran into Reigate there was what would now be called the stockbroker belt. In fact there were very few stockbrokers but they were for the most part, prosperous businessmen commuting to London each day. Almost without exception they possessed large well built detached houses, usually with beautifully kept gardens and sometimes with private tennis courts. On the other side of the London-Brighton road was a very densely populated area, mostly of terraced houses. Here lived the followers, if not the descendants, of those who had engineered and built the Brighton line more than a hundred years ago. They had their own mission church and its faithful adherents, but with a few shining exceptions I never found this section of the parish particularly welcoming.

I defy anyone, however gifted or charming, to weld together in any real way these three strands of society. Naturally I had friends in all three sections, but to get them to meet and make friends with each other was another matter altogether.

A further factor which made a chilling difference in atmosphere to me was the plain fact that this parish had never been for months together in common peril. Their sole bomb damage, as far as I could see, was caused by a flying bomb shot down by one of our pilots over open ground and unfortunately plunging to earth near Earlswood station. This nasty accident was still hotly resented.

Moreover, since for over four years I had been conducting services in a flimsy shell of a building I was horrified to discover the fear which was caused by the sound of the siren upon a congregation in a church of solid stone, whose walls were in some places *nine feet thick*. Only one such siren sounded after I moved to Redhill and this was at the time of the morning service. I was disgusted to find that most of the congregation poured out of the doors and headed for the hastily constructed shelters dug out on Redhill Common, where they were, I think, far more vulnerable.

The daily grind of parish work

Although I had, to begin with, the faithful assistance of the Reverend D. A. P. Shiels, the sheer routine work was hard and long. To maintain services in three places of worship every Sunday was in itself hard work, but in addition, for me, I had to go every Sunday afternoon, and also on Christmas Day, to the Royal Earlswood Institution. No doubt things are different now, but in those days mongols, spastics and the mentally subnormal were all treated with never failing kindness but with much the same overall care. I do remember the infinite care and patience which was given to the more intelligent spastic children, but my general feeling was that the run-of-the-mill mental deficient was treated somewhat anonymously. This task, and I must say I was always made embarrassingly welcome either on Sunday or during the week, was removed from my shoulders soon after the National Health Service was introduced. A full-time chaplain was appointed for the county hospital and its offshoot at Smallfields a few miles away, and he also served the Royal Earlswood Institution.

At all times the faithful men and women who supported each of the three places of worship gave me unstinted loyalty. And I had in addition a remarkable headmaster of the church school. His name was R. G. Bennett and, in addition to being an exceptionally good head, he was a qualified lay reader and was always ready to help me in conducting services. He, alas, died soon after his retirement at the age of sixty, not very long after I had left. I shall always be grateful to him, not least for a period of eight months when I had no curate at all and sometimes felt ready to die from overwork.

However, I did manage to secure another curate, newly ordained from Lincoln theological college. His name was Frank Bowles and, although he was ready with plenty of quiet criticism of my methods of ministry, he gave me hundreds of hours of faithful assistance for over three years. He had a great concern for people and considerable organising ability. This

103

was shown later when he accepted an important living in the diocese of Leicester. He and his wife were doing a great work there, and I was horrified to hear of his death in the prime of his ministry.

Although the chief enemy in that parish was sheer impenetrable apathy, this does not mean that full use was not made of the church for baptisms, marriages and funerals. I did not reckon up the total of baptisms, but of the weddings, I myself conducted some 600 such ceremonies in the ten years I spent at St. John's. When one considers that I interviewed all these couples, twice at least before the ceremony itself, here was a tiring, though rewarding, ministry in itself.

An eventful year of victory

The church was struck by lightning in the spring of 1945. It made a noise not unlike that of a detonating bomb and did considerable damage to the building internally. All the gas-pipes (long since disused) were ripped out and two perfectly innocent loudspeakers (used at one time, I imagine, for some form of public address) which were not connected to anything were destroyed as if by a physical blow. It was therefore decided to have the lightning conductor repaired and have the weather-cock re-gilded at the same time. No one had been to the top of the spire (185 feet) since the church was built in the middle of the nineteenth century and I was told that the weather-cock would prove to be as large as a donkey. The steeplejack who undertook the work told me that it had been his ambition to scale the spire since he was a boy. This was understandable but my heart was in my mouth when, after erecting his series of ladders, and removing the weather-cock (which after all was no bigger than a large dog) he re-ascended and ate his picnic lunch sitting on the mounting which had supported the cock.

I remember this well because the ladders were still in position on V.J. Day (V.E. Day had passed off with services of thanksgiving but little other outward rejoicing). The local authorities decided to floodlight the church and very splendid it looked. Hundreds came to walk round and admire, and I was told that the illuminated church was visible for nearly forty miles. This is quite likely to be true since the building itself is set on a small hill some 600 feet above sea level. I think this height was also the reason for the coldness of the winters.

The floodlighting was so impressive that I think many of us would have liked it to be installed permanently, to be used at least in the winter months, but the cost was prohibitive. I remember, during the week or so that the illumination was on, being approached by several young men for permission to climb the spire since the ladders were still in position. I said, "Certainly you can, but entirely at your own risk." In fact nobody ever went more than about some twenty feet above ground.

With the lifting of the black-out I discovered that there was no external lighting for the church at all. Since most of the parochial church council never attended evensong they did not appreciate the inconvenience and even the danger of approaching the building by way of either some steep steps, or, more popularly, by a stony slope. It took all my persuasive powers to have at least some external lights fitted. The electrician who drilled a hole for a light to be fitted at the west end of the church took nearly all day to pierce the solid stone. It was he who informed me that the wall was nine feet thick.

The number of communicants slowly began to increase and so did the size of the congregations. But, apart from the slowly growing number of the faithful, I felt surrounded by a wall of invincible indifference. I remember, for example, sending out fifty personal invitations to men to attend a meeting where we might freely discuss the relevance of the Christian faith to the post-war world. No one turned up for the meeting and no one even had the courtesy to refuse politely.

The youth fellowship was similarly daunting. Perhaps I was getting a little old, at forty, to attempt to lead these young people, but the methods which had been so successful in Lee fell completely flat in Redhill. Even a visit from my young friends from my former parish failed to raise a glimmer of response.

A warning from the future

In the parish magazine for March, 1946, I expressed my concern about the church in the fictitious newspaper article purporting to be from the *Surrey Times* issue dated February 29th, 1986.

Continuing my tour of the churches of this borough I paid a visit on Sunday evening to St. John's, Redhill. What a magnificent building it is, although even to the casual eye it is obviously badly in need of repair. As I made my way through the churchyard, terribly neglected and overgrown, alas, I could not help thinking with longing of the days when churches were able to afford a verger.

The church was very cold, indeed it has not been heated since 1978, and it was very dimly lighted. I imagine that, like so many others, St. John's has to exercise the most rigid economy. The congregation consisted of three elderly ladies, one elderly man, and myself. We sat almost in the front pew, and behind us was a curtain extending right across the church, and in consequence we did not feel quite so small a gathering in such a large building.

The vicar conducted the service reverently and well, although it is a pity that nowadays we have to do without the music of the organ. (I may say in passing that in the good old days St. John's had a first-class organist and if only the organ could be cleaned and repaired it would still sound very well.)

As I sat and listened to the vicar's excellent sermon, part of my mind wandered off and visualised this fine church as it must have been in the days when there was a robed choir and the many pews were full of worshippers. I could not help speculating as to why our lovely churches have become very little more than museum pieces. Afterwards, in the vestry, I tackled the vicar about this matter. I found him remarkable cheerful. "Things are improving," he said. "Last year I had four baptisms, and I have managed to get three little girls and one boy for my Sunday school. Naturally," he added with a smile, "I myself am the teaching staff. You see," he went on, "I believe in getting hold of the children and young people and training them as members of God's church." For a moment his eyes grew wistful. "If only," he said sadly, "they had made a real effort, say forty years ago, to win the young then, in those critical years after the Second World War, we might have filled our churches with them and their children today but . . ."

Doing all the epistles

C. S.Lewis had written, "I hope very much you will carry out your plan of doing all the epistles." By setting aside one morning a week of my busy schedule at St. John's, Redhill, I had by 1946 finished all the epistles. C. S. Lewis suggested the title, *Letters to Young Churches*. I sent it round to several publishers, all of whom sent it back, firmly and politely, with a rejection slip. Then armed with a letter from C. S. Lewis, I sent it to his publisher, Geoffrey Bles:

4th Feb. 1946

St. John's Vicarage,
Redhill,
Surrey

Dear Sir,

I am sending you herewith part of a new free translation of the Letters of the New Testament. I am, of course, aware that there are already several modern versions, but to me, at any rate, they nearly always read as palpable translations. They are often so concerned with giving exact verbal equivalents for Greek words that they lose freshness and spontaneity, and lack the sense of being live letters written to real people.

I have been encouraged to continue the work, which has taken the spare time of three years, by the remarks of Mr. C. S. Lewis, to whom I sent a copy of the "Letter to Colossae", the first which I attempted to turn into modern idiom. Mr. Lewis wrote:

"Thank you a hundred times. I thought I knew Colossians pretty well, but your paraphrase made it far more significant . . . it was like seeing a familiar picture after it's been cleaned . . ."

107

Parts of the typescript have been used, and in one case incorporated into a play, by youth fellowships in various parts of the country, and the enthusiastic reception they received and the keen interest aroused have encouraged me to approach you with a view to their publication.

My aim has been to make these letters both intelligible and readable. The reader may then, his interest being quickened, turn for closer study to the more scholarly translations. I am sure that there is a large number of people who have been "put off" the study of the N. T. epistles by the undeniably beautiful but obscure Authorised Version, and who need something in the modern idiom, easily read, to make them see the relevance of the N.T.'s message today.

How far I have succeeded you will, of course, be able to judge, and if you consider the version worth publication I should naturally be very glad to discuss the matter further.

Yours faithfully,

Geoffrey Bles was quite interested and invited me to have lunch with him in London. Eventually he agreed to publish the work, especially if we could get a commendatory foreword from Lewis. This was readily forthcoming, for he was always generous. *Letters to Young Churches* was published in October 1947. It was no doubt his commendation, and the title, which he suggested, which launched the book on its way. It was a slow starter (were there not already translations such as Weymouth, Moffat and Knox?) and I have an interesting letter from the late Geoffrey Bles telling me that "rather more than 1,300 copies" had been sold in the previous nine months. He thought this was very good. Little did he, or I, guess that within two years or so the sales of the "Letters" would exceed that figure every *week*.

Success
Part of this rocketing success was due to personal recommendation by such people as Dr. Wand, Bishop Huddleston, Dr. Mervyn Stockwood, Professor C. F. D. Moule and many

other prominent Christian authorities. I also enjoyed most favourable reviews from the *Church Times*, the *Church of England Newspaper*, the *Methodist Recorder*, and the *Life of Faith*. The *Times Literary Supplement* treated my work most kindly and before long favourable notices were appearing in the general secular press, both national and provincial.

But, in terms of numbers, the huge acceleration of sales began in 1948 when the *Living Church* (Episcopalian U.S.A.) gave me an enormous boost, beginning with the words, "Now and again a book appears that is an event, and such an event has occurred this spring in the appearance of J. B. Phillips' *Letters to Young Churches.*" In a matter of weeks I was being reviewed in publications of virtually every denomination from coast to coast, almost always in terms of highest praise. And then began the flow of letters from the U.S.A. and Canada, nearly always appreciative, which went on for twenty years.

Jennifer

But I have allowed the explosive success of *Letters to Young Churches* to carry me on, chronologically, too far. My wife, who had two disappointing miscarriages, began to produce another infant. We have often said, jokingly, that our daughter, Jennifer, was a most expensive baby. This was because she was born in 1946, two years before the National Health Service, and my wife needed special treatment to avoid a further miscarriage. This pre-natal work, and the birth itself, were looked after devotedly by Dr. Kathleen Muir, one of our most faithful supporters in the church. This fine woman is now dead, alas, but we shall always be grateful to her for her care and skill. (The little red-haired babe, born in the early hours of Monday morning May 20th, 1946, is now happily married to Roger Croft with two children of her own, David and James.)

It is curious how the mind works. I am by nature rather a highly strung type always prone to anxiety. I thought that after I had taken my wife safely to the nursing home that I should spend hours pacing up and down, possibly smoking innumerable cigarettes. In fact, after a few minutes of prayer, I lay down and fell into a deep sleep. I think I must have been dreaming about twins, for when Kathleen Muir rang me to say that I had a daughter and that my wife was well I am told that my reply was, "Is that all?"

8

St. John's, Redhill
1945–1954

I once asked a group of young people to answer quickly, without thinking too much, the following question – "Do you think God understands Radio-location?" Several of them said "No", and then of course laughed as they realised what they were saying. But that quick answer confirmed what I suspected, and in many of their minds lurked an idea of God as the old gentleman in the sky, somewhat old-fashioned and a little bewildered by modern progress. We need to give in this scientific age an idea of God really big and wide and high. Science, which many almost worship, is really only re-discovering the thoughts of God and personally I think it would do good if in Bibles and prayer books, we not only had religious pictures but photographs also of such things as the spiral nebulae and the Milky Way.

A busy parish

The continual work at St. John's, Redhill, as I look back on it now seems a hard grind, and indeed it was. But I trained myself and my curates never to let anyone see that one might be conducting the sixth service of the day. To them it was important, and the spirit of freshness and vitality must, as I learned from Gilly, at all times be preserved.

In those ten years the thing which cheered me most deeply was the growing habit of the parochial church council to use the beautiful lady chapel for private prayer before our actual meetings. Before I left I think everybody was making this a habit, and I am quite sure that our meetings progressed with much more smoothness and agreed sense of purpose than they had in the years before.

Looking back through the "vicar's letters" of the first year or so at Redhill I see that I had a good deal to criticise, a good many weaknesses to point out and some earnest appeals to make for service to the church. Some of the parishioners must have thought that the vicar was always grumbling. Any incumbent will tend to do this but he has to beware of too much scolding. I was able in August 1946 to record signs of encouragement:

> I have been immensely cheered by the spontaneous form-ing of a study group of "men of St. John's". These men are concerned at the drift from the church, the collapse of religious faith and of moral standards. They are prepared to spend time, not merely in talk, but in thinking out practical ways of forwarding the Kingdom of Christ among men. They have not set themselves an easy task, and it will probably be weeks or months before they get to the stage of action. But they are, to me at any rate, a most encouraging sign – that the laymen are seeing that the work of the church *cannot* be left merely to the clergy and a few devoted workers. All laymen whose faith is a real thing to them must be prepared to do something for their church. The whole conception of the church is beginning to change, it is to be a centre of *self-giving*, not only a convenient place for receiv-ing.

Within a year the women's discussion group made a good start.

Prayer and healing

In my last four years we ran (by post because of the scattered nature of the parish) a monthly prayer circle leaflet. I suppose there were not quite a hundred members, but it was heartening to know that such a number was praying regularly for the needs of the parish. Among them was a splendid Christian who I am sure will not mind if I call her by her Christian name, Olive. It transpired that she was not only a

woman of prayer and deep spiritual insight but also possessed the gift of healing. She was very reticent about this and
would normally only lay hands on anyone who was sick if she
strongly felt that it was God's will for her to do so.

I well remember being present when Olive laid hands upon
a middle-aged man with an inoperable cancer. Within a week
I saw with my own eyes that the growth had disappeared, and
the doctors soon pronounced him fit. He lived for another
twenty years after that. This man was a good husband and
father, but I would not say that he was a man of especially
robust faith. At the same time of his particularly malignant
disease there lay another man, this time one of strong and
active faith, in terrible pain through cancer of some part of the
spine. I used to visit him, pray with him and generally try to
keep up his courage. Finally I decided to persuade Olive to lay
hands on him. Surely what God had accomplished with one
sufferer He could do with another? Olive took a lot of persua-
sion but she did finally lay hands on the tormented man with
the spinal cancer. Faith was certainly present, but nothing
even by way of temporary relief was granted, and in another
two weeks the sufferer was dead.

Despite my ensuing bewilderment (which continues to this
day) I was myself persuaded to lay hands on those who asked
for it in a brief service which followed the Wednesday morning celebration of holy communion. I have no gift of healing
myself (except for that extraordinary case in my first parish)
and I did this as Christ's representative, possibly as an
ordained man I might be a channel of his healing power.
Nothing dramatic happened, but I do know of several people
who felt their tensions relax and their normal attitude to life
change from one of fear to one of faith, which is in itself a kind
of miracle. And I also remember one old lady, who was
constantly in terrible pain, telling me in a wholly uncharacter-
istically sweet voice that she "had no more pain". A few
weeks later she died peacefully and serenely with no recur-
rence of her agonies.

I have no doubt at all that God *does* heal people through the
agency of certain gifted persons, but I am still more than a little
puzzled by the apparently sporadic distribution of the gift,

and the apparently capricious way of its working. I have also become convinced that a good deal of nonsense is spoken and written about healing. There are meetings where fit youngish healers have by sheer force of personality persuaded trembling old ladies that they were healed. (Of course if they relapsed afterwards it was because of their own lack of faith.) By all means let the subject be studied without prejudice but let the healers practise with scrupulous honesty as well as with compassion.

Broadcasting

I think it must have been about 1948 that I was invited, with some dozen others, for an audition at Broadcasting House in London. In those days I had no tape-recorder and, like everyone else, was surprised at the reproduction of my own voice. I had for years made a practice of listening to myself while preaching or speaking so that my diction should be as clear as I could make it. But I was quite unprepared for the comparative deep voice that I apparently possessed. When one comes to think about it no man ever hears his own voice as others do. He mostly hears through the vibrations that pass through his skull and these do not include notes of the lower register. Anyway, along with several others, I was approved. I remember being told that my voice was free from accent of any kind, which I took, rightly or wrongly, to be a compliment.

It was in 1949 that I was invited to conduct four Sunday "people's services" in what was then the Light Programme. I believe these were quite successful; they certainly led to an unexpectedly large correspondence. The Reverend John Williams, who helped and encouraged me in these first efforts at broadcast communication, advised me never to think of the possible millions who might be listening, but to imagine that I was talking to a small friendly group. I am sure this is good advice and I have tried to follow it ever since.

The Religious Broadcasting Department of the B.B.C.

In 1952 I was given the privilege of acting as chaplain to the B.B.C.'s Religious Broadcasting Department at its annual conference, to be held that year at St. Julian's, a retreat house in deepest Sussex. I enjoyed those few days enormously and once again experienced the peculiar thrill of meeting men more gifted and highly trained than I. Francis House was then head of religious broadcasting, while Edwin Robertson (a man of fantastic linguistic and organising ability) was assistant head. I have remained in contact with Edwin over various projects for nearly thirty years, and we still find each other's company stimulating. I clearly remember also Richard Tatlock, then in charge of Light Programme broadcasts, Cyril Taylor, a musician to his finger-tips, and later precentor of Salisbury Cathedral, and the late Martin Wilson, then religious broadcasting organiser in the west. I felt strongly drawn to him, and with one of my rare intuitions about the future, ventured to say to him that we should see a lot of one another in the years to come. He replied, "I don't see why; you're centred in Surrey and my headquarters are in Bristol." Nevertheless what I had felt so strongly came true, and both professionally in the matter of broadcasting, as well as in the friendship of two Christians struggling with the presentation of the Christian faith in a world of bewildering change, we developed a deep and lasting friendship. At the same conference I met, and liked immediately, the overseas religious broadcasting organiser, the Reverend W. D. Kennedy-Bell, a quiet modest man, if ever there was one. In the mere few minutes he was allotted he outlined what he was doing to cover his vast parish which extended almost all over the world. He had, and has, one of the most beautiful speaking voices I have ever heard. Ronald Falconer, that stalwart from Scotland, was also there and lucidly presented the particular problems that faced broadcasting in that land of a few big cities and innumerable scattered small communities. The Midlands regional representative was Maurice Dean. He was the immediate predecessor of William Purcell, whom I later got to know and regard with affection and admiration. Peter Hamilton represented the north region. I also remember a fellow guest, the Reverend Kenneth Henderson, the man in charge of religious broadcasting for the Australian Broadcasting Commission. We made friendly contact and I later recorded several tapes for broadcasting in his country.

Apart from Francis House's secretary, a merry hearted girl, called Margaret, and the Reverend Elsie Chamberlain I can only remember one other woman present in that company. She was Katharine Trevelyan, a writer of some distinction, and she made useful contributions to our discussions, as well as giving us a wholly delightful lecture.

Television was only an infant then, but we listened to a well informed lecture from George Barnes, then director of T.V. Broadcasting (later Sir George Barnes).

Billy Graham

I think it was in 1952 that I received a visit from Dr. Billy Graham with his charming and intelligent wife. "I want to thank you, Dr. Phillips," he began, "for *Letters to Young Churches*." "Don't you think," I retorted, "that you really mean that you want to thank Paul, John, James and Peter? I didn't write the letters you know." There was a perceptible pause, then he chuckled. "Why, sure, sure." And we had a long and most interesting conversation. He admitted to me that he knew very well that he should "go right back to College", but the demands on him as an evangelist were so pressing that he never seemed to have the time. More the pity! There is no doubt at all of Dr. Graham's personal charm and sincerity nor of the force of his preaching. But there appeared to me certain large gaps in his knowledge of the world in which the human predicament is set.

There were two people I knew whose decision to lead the Christian life was certainly influenced by the Graham crusade. One was a young actor who had become typecast by playing on stage and in film the part of the "Wilmslow Boy". The other was a young painter of some distinction and her conversion was a wholehearted affair. I am sure she would not mind my telling you that she intended to give her integrity as an artist to Jesus Christ. It was a difficult decision for her for she came from a strongly atheistic background. I have no doubt that she had to face ridicule, the loss of certain friends and the beginning of a new life in the fellowship of the church. I had a letter from her years later reminding me of how lonely she felt as I baptised her in St. John's, Redhill, and yet what happiness and satisfaction she had found in the work and company of Christian people.

Coronation Year was soon upon us and she, my young artist friend, transformed the internal beauty of St. John's by painting the whole of the wrought-iron screen in the Coronation colours. We also enjoyed the special musical treat of a visit by the St. Martin's Singers, led at the time by my friend the Reverend W. D. Kennedy-Bell.

Staff

By this time I had two first-rate curates, Pat Simpson and Norman Mantle. Both these young men were active and efficient. Pat showed himself able to infuse some life into our young people and led all kinds of projects, including the successful production of a passion play on the church. He was a vigorous preacher. Norman also spoke well, more quietly but effectively, but he really came into his own when a new housing estate was built in the fields surrounding Meadvale. It seemed that almost every week new families with young children arrived in the area, and Norman made them his great concern. Between them these two young men were of the greatest help to me, and slowly but surely something approaching spiritual life began to seep back into the church.

Another part of my life which required hard work and discipline was the matter of translation. I had decided that I could not spare more than one morning a week on this demanding task. At the same time having failed to find a satisfactory replacement for our retired verger, we engaged Margery Hopkins to take on the verger's work. This she tackled with great energy and determination. The church was spotless, the communion plate and linen were always beautifully clean, and the registers were impeccably kept. In addition Margery agreed to do some of my secretarial work, and I paid out of my own pocket fifty pounds a year for her services on Tuesday mornings, since this was not strictly parish work. She was most reliable and competent, and helped enormously during my latter years at Redhill.

The vicar's wife

Through all the years of our marriage my wife has been utterly loyal, even undertaking such unlikely (to her) tasks as running the mothers' union. She was always there when wanted, and the dread of calling at the vicarage (inherited from heaven knows what far-off days) was dissipated by her kindly approach to the timid caller ringing at the doorbell. We often had unexpected visitors but she never failed to cope with their needs. To me she was, and is, an invaluable friend as well as an incorruptible critic. The very fact that she came from a non-churchy background helped me many times to see life as it is, and not necessarily through the spectacles of an Anglican vicar.

Making men whole

In 1952 I was also invited to be speaker at the church missionary society's summer school, to be held that year at Bangor, on the north west coast of Wales. It was a very happy school and I made many friends of widely different nationalities. The chosen theme was "Making Men Whole", and the daily talks, after a little judicious editing, were published under that title later in the same year.

Experiences in the hospital

After the appointment of a chaplain to the Redhill County Hospital by the national health service, I suppose, strictly speaking, I could have completely given up my visits there. But I found, in practice, that the chaplain was by no means always able to cover the ground, and since the hospital was within my parish, I continued to visit one afternoon a week. Naturally one avoided the elementary mistakes of staying too long with someone who had just come round from an anaesthetic or who was in severe pain. At the same time experience taught me when someone was longing for someone to talk to, and sometimes to find those to whom any form of illness or weakness had hitherto been a stranger. Some of the latter sort were surprisingly frightened and bewildered and were trying to think out afresh the problem of life, pain and the existence of God. I found hospital visiting a rewarding, if somewhat exhausting, experience.

One afternoon I went into one of the women's wards to find a dozen patients either sitting on, or standing close to the bed of one particular patient. There was much laughter so I asked to be allowed to share the joke. At this all the patients, except the one lying down, scuttled back to their own beds like naughty schoolgirls. "Well," I said with mock severity, "and what have you been up to?" The woman, somewhere in her forties, gave me a rather wry smile. "Well, I was reading their hands," she said. "All right, then," said I, "read mine," and gave her my right hand. I would emphasise that this was a county hospital and drew its patients from various parts of Surrey. This woman was not a parishioner of mine (she lived some miles away) and had never seen me before in her life. At once, with little or no hesitation, she began to tell me some of the salient points of my past life and to tell me of my present hopes and fears. This was, to say the least of it, uncanny and I said, "Right! Now tell me what I was thinking as I walked up the stairs to this ward." Without hesitation she told me that I had been worrying about a new car. This was perfectly true. Our old banger was on its last legs and I was only too conscious of the cost of a new one. Yet to run this scattered parish without a reliable car was an impossibility. But how could this woman, a complete stranger, know what was bothering me?

I pressed her for an explanation. "It's a matter of reading people's thoughts," she said simply. "Of course I don't read hands but the fact of holding someone's hand usually makes their thoughts clearer to me." She went on to explain that she had had this gift all her adult life, and that it was sometimes embarrassing. Naturally it was easier with some people than with others. "I would never use this gift for *money*," she declared emphatically. "All I was doing just now was for a bit of fun because the girls were a bit bored." Further conversation revealed that she was a sincere Christian and she had no explanation to offer for her unusual gift.

E.S.P.

I have known the gift of telepathy only a few times in my life. But I had one brilliant example of its powers operating in me that I can never forget. A great friend of mine, Eric, was director of a music store, with branches in both Reigate and Redhill. We had become, and still are, friends, and at this time I knew that his wife was expecting her third child. It so happened that I was driving my daughter to her little pre-prep school in Reigate when I passed Eric on his way to his office there. He gave me the thumbs up sign, and I immediately knew that the new-born child was a boy and that his name was Nigel. As soon as I got back to the vicarage I telephoned Eric and said, "Congratulations on the birth of Nigel." "My God," he replied in what I can only describe as a voice of awe, "how did you know?" Indeed, how did I know? We had never on any occasion even speculated about the sex of the baby-to-be, still less talked about names. Sundry less dramatic examples of telepathy have happened between Eric and me over the last twenty years, but neither of us will ever forget that one.

Cleaning the roof

Among the unusual, and happy memories, of my time at Redhill is the curious method we adopted to clean the inside of the roof, some fifty-five feet high. The normal method of cleaning would have meant expensive scaffolding and a considerable labour bill. I thought that hydrogen-filled balloons might help us to do the task. Ex-R.A.F. meteorological balloons, some five feet in diameter, were cheaply obtainable at surplus stores. The British Oxygen Company supplied us with hydrogen free of charge, and we found that four balloons had plenty of lifting power to take brooms and brushes to the height required. Steering by light wooden booms was a little tricky, but a small team of us soon learnt to do it. The spiders' webs and general dust of over a hundred years were quickly brought down and sucked up by a vacuum cleaner. This, as far as I know, original method featured in the late lamented *Picture Post* as well as in other weekly and daily papers. Churches were cleaned in this way in many places, even in far away Australia.

The organist

My organist for the first few years at Redhill had been Philip Bornet, an accomplished musician. I don't remember the exact year of his departure but he emigrated, with his wife, his children and aged mother, to Christchurch, New Zealand. Here he did some notable work before succumbing to a stroke.

His successor was Frank Goodey, a most remarkable man for he was totally blind. His musicianship was superb and his memory fantastic. Merely to think of memorising every psalm and its modern pointing makes my head reel. Frank Goodey possessed absolute pitch and could tell if an L.P. record were as little as a quarter of a tone flat by the end of its playing. He found his way about the parish by tapping such things as metal lamp-posts, each of which had, to him, a distinct and recognisable musical note. He had never heard high-fidelity reproduction until he heard mine. I remember that he flushed with pleasure. "It's as though heavy curtains have been drawn back," he exclaimed. And then went on, "It may seem a strange thing to say but it's like looking at people without their clothes on." It *was* a strange thing for a completely blind man to say, but I think I know what he meant. There is an extraordinary sense of actual presence when sound is reproduced accurately.

No one would have guessed that Frank Goodey was blind. The only practical difference it made to me was that the little red and green lights which I had installed over the organ console (to warn the organist of the arrival of the bride at a wedding, for example) had to be replaced with a quiet high-pitched buzzer. When we broadcast, a touch on the shoulder was all he needed as warning that we were on the air. He was a cheerful entertaining man and a most gifted teacher. I am sorry to have lost touch with him over the years.

The church school

I have already mentioned our church school and its fine headmaster R. G. Bennett. The school was perched on the side of Redhill Common only a few hundred yards from the church. This made it easily possible for the boys of the school to attend church for special occasions on weekdays. It was also very handy for me, the vicar, to drop in and occasionally to teach. But then a blow fell. We were told, I think as early as 1952, that as the building was old and did not reach modern standards a new church school should be built. This meant many months of arguing and discussing, visits to and from the county hall, and a search to find a new site for a brand-new modern school. No site could be found within the parish boundaries, for all the open space still not built upon was common land. Finally it was decided by Surrey county council that the new site should be about a mile and a half away, in the parish of St. Luke's, Reigate. Very reluctantly and not without some hard feelings we had to bow to the inevitable. Under the arrangements then in force we had to find half the cost of the building (less of course what the old property would fetch) and the state would pay the other half. How we raised the not inconsiderable sum I cannot remember in any detail. I do remember that all kinds of special efforts were made and that a number of individuals gave most generously. Fortunately for him, I think, the opening of the new building came soon after Mr. Bennett's retirement. It was a fine new building and we appointed an exceptionally good headmaster, Mr. F. Boddington. But distance snapped the close links between church and school, as we knew it was bound to do. There was no public transport between the two places, and although the new St. John's Boys School has built up for itself a high reputation, its link with present-day members of St. John's congregation is slender indeed.

The most infuriating part of the whole bureaucratic method is that after the new school was built the county authorities re-furbished the obsolete buildings (a thing which they had assured us was impossible) and, when I last heard, had re-opened it as a state school!

Translating the gospels

By 1952, still working on Tuesday mornings only, I had completed the translation of the gospels, and they were met with a warm welcome, which I found very cheering. The work itself was in a way not hard since I know Greek pretty well and had had, since 1948, a more reliable Greek text. But I should say that, on average, every verse in both the "letters" and the "gospels" was revised some seven or eight times. My long-suffering family and friends put up with a great deal in hearing it read again and again. Perhaps I might outline some of my own principles – I look upon a translator as a kind of liaison officer between what was written long ago and the people of today. On the one hand he must try and understand the Greek that was written in the first place, but it's just as important that he should understand the thought forms of people for whom he is writing today. Now, I know that some people think that I have thereby lowered the level of the literary quality of the gospels; I don't honestly think that's so. The examples they credit to me are very unconvincing. It is important to understand the way people are thinking. There's no such person as the man in the street; but there is a manner of thought, a sort of shape of thinking which does exist among the majority of people for whom I at least was writing.

To me it is also very important to avoid – what shall I call it – not a holy style exactly, but the style of legend. It's a temptation for those of us who have been parsons for years to impart a sort of holy reverent flavour to the whole thing. And that we just must not do. We have to translate in a matter-of-fact style because these are matters of fact. Otherwise you get the sense that this is a beautiful story, and how lovely it sounds. An effect produced very beautifully by the Authorised Version; but that is not what I am after. These men were writing down things which were actual facts within living memory of people, of their contemporaries, and it is important then to get across to the men and women of today that these were facts.

Sometimes you have to give a little bit of a paraphrase because of the extraordinary economy of phrase by the gospel writers. After the temptation of our Lord in the wilderness, for example, we read in St. Mark's gospel: "And he hungered" or "He was an hungered", as the Authorised Version says. Well, if you put that into contemporary English: "He was without food for forty days and forty nights, and afterwards he was hungry," it sounds funny; it sounds like one of those masterpieces of understatement for which English people are supposed to be renowned. And so I had to alter that to: "He felt very hungry," which doesn't produce that sense of semi-humorous anti-climax. And then again we're so accustomed to exaggerations in our ordinary speech. I have sometimes, for instance, said, "vast crowds followed him" when the Greek only says, "crowds followed him," because I'm afraid by our modern usage we have debased words; we need to have things somewhat exaggerated and somewhat underlined in order to make this equivalent effect on the modern reader as was produced in the first case in the minds of those for whom the gospels were first written.

Of course all this led to a lot of correspondence both in this country and then, mountingly, in the U.S.A. Correspondents also wrote from Canada, Australia and New Zealand. Very few of these hundreds were purely fan-mail; many of them raised important questions of translation and interpretation. All of them were answered as well as I knew how.

In December 1953 at the invitation of Edwin Robertson at the B.B.C. I broadcast a discussion on the art of translation with Dr. E. V. Rieu. He had recently translated the four gospels into modern English for Penguin Books. The joy of the occasion was its "unscripted" nature. We could talk as long as we liked and then the Third Programme could edit the tape-recording to suit their timetable. Fortunately, I think, Dr. Rieu and I became friends almost at once and the longish talk never showed signs of becoming a slanging match between two rival translators.

Your God is too small

I had also written, for the Epworth Press (since Geoffrey Bles had declined it) a small book called *Your God is Too Small*, and this was published in 1952. I wrote it because it was obvious to me that many people had far too little and narrow a conception of God. Their faith was small because, frankly, modern life and modern ideas had long ago outstripped their childish and rather primitive notions. Rather to my surprise the book was a huge success – selling over 130,000 copies in Britain alone and being translated into German and other

European languages. To judge from my correspondence it is still read and appreciated today, more than twenty years later.

Broadcast services from Redhill

During the last few years at Redhill, we produced three more broadcast services. Two were made for the overseas service of the B.B.C. at the request of Kennedy-Bell. I remember the murmurings of a few malcontents who didn't see why we should produce services which could not be heard in this country. But most of the choir and congregation rallied round splendidly and regarded it as an honour and a responsibility into which we should put our best efforts.

The last broadcast we made from St. John's was at the invitation of Cyril Taylor. It was made on St. Mark's day, 1953, and the theme of my address was the value of Mark's gospel, which I had translated less than two years before. Cyril Taylor was, and probably is, a perfectionist but he wrote me a charming letter of thanks and appreciation afterwards. I think we probably acquitted ourselves quite well. I was, as always, enormously impressed by the meticulous care taken by the B.B.C. sound engineers to preserve proper balance of voice and music, and to adjust telephone lines to receive and transmit the "signal".

Tracts for our times

We enjoyed in the Reigate deanery a very happy chapter, largely I think because there were no extremists of any Anglican party among us. At one of these meetings I remember speaking at some length to Canon Gordon Hewitt (then secretary of the Lutterworth Press, which had been evacuated to Redhill from London). He maintained that although the Lutterworth Press was the old religious tract society no one could write tracts acceptable for modern times. I could not let this pass and eventually wrote over twenty Lutterworth leaflets, each illustrated by a humorous drawing, and bearing provocative titles such as, "The Comfort of the Atom Bomb", "Are you a Man or a Mouse?", "The Dumb Blonde", "I always keep an Open Mind" etc. The aim was that each pithily worded tract should present, in modern parlance, one part or other of the Christian message. The leaflets sold over a million copies in various parts of the world, and were used in many thousands in the mission to the R.A.F., which took place, I think near the end of the war, or possibly just after it. Eventually the tracts were published as a book, rather against my own advice, and it was called *Is God at Home?* Although the small book had sold quite well both here and in the U.S.A. I am still dubious of the value of collecting together rather disparate tracts and publishing them as a book.

Sermons from the Acts

The only other broadcasting which I undertook in 1953 was to write, at the invitation of Edwin Robertson, imaginatively expanded versions of Peter's speech at the day of Pentecost, Stephen's speech before his martyrdom, Paul's speech on Mars Hill and his defence before King Agrippa. For these four broadcasts on the Third Programme I read the run in while the speeches themselves were read by men of the calibre of Norman Shelley, Alan Wheatley, Carleton Hobbs and Hallam Fordham. I thought the professionals did their work splendidly, and I must confess that I am sorry that the only place where the speeches can be found today is at the end of my separately published translation of the Acts, called the *Young Church in Action*.

9

The First American Tour
1954

In 1952 a small group of Presbyterians from Hollywood visited us to our mutual delight and profit. They invited me to address some thousands of young people at a Christian conference to be held at a retreat centre called Forest Home 5,000 feet up in the mountains around Los Angeles. This was to be held in August 1954 and I agreed to accept their kind invitation.

Leaving Redhill

By the beginning of 1954, my tenth year at Redhill, I was becoming more and more aware that I could not properly run a parish as large as St. John's and at the same time pursue a career as a writer, lecturer and occasional broadcaster. The correspondence itself was beginning to escalate, as my American friends would say, and I resolved that I would complete ten years as vicar of St. John's, and then find a quiet centre where I could write and from which I could emerge to speak, preach, lecture or broadcast. I took the advice of two bishops and this is precisely what they advised. It so happened that years before, realising that one day we should have to retire, we had purchased a small plot almost "for a song" in Swanage. So we planned to build a house there, using the services of a Mr. Joel who had been chief architect of the new St. John's church school. The utmost secrecy was observed throughout as I did not want to announce my impending departure until the very end of 1954, or possibly early in 1955 to complete my ten years exactly.

1954 was indeed a strenuous year. I, and the parish generally, knew that I should be away in Hollywood during August and September for some four weeks in all.

We had to make plans for our new house, and sneak down to Swanage to see, at least, that the foundations were laid. I was more than ever grateful to my two colleagues Norman and Pat, whom I could trust perfectly to maintain the proper working of the parish while I was away.

U.S.A.

I knew that the visit to the U.S.A. in the late summer of 1954 would be something of an ordeal, but it was not until I got there that I realised how strenuous was the programme. In the meantime I prepared with some care a series of lectures on "New Testament Christianity". These lectures, with a little editing, were subsequently published under that title by Hodders of London and Macmillan of New York.

In mid-August our little party of four (myself, my wife, our eight-year-old daughter and secretary Margery) embarked on the *Queen Elizabeth*. Not one of us had ever been on a big liner before and we were duly impressed by everything, the cinema, the swimming-pool and the excellent food. The five-day trip seemed all too short and before we had really had time to settle in we found ourselves re-packing for disembarkation. Of course we were up in the bows ready to see the Statue of Liberty and the first skyscrapers we had ever seen. Certainly they were impressive, but I suppose because we had seen the skyline of New York many times before at the cinema, the whole scene was predictable. Macmillans were to be our hosts for a few days before we flew on to Los Angeles. They sent their representatives to get us swiftly through the customs and held a splendid tea-party for us. There I had the chance of meeting my religious editor, Guy Brown. He must have been of enormous value to that firm. Not only was he an unbelievably hard worker, reading typescripts far into the night and sometimes through whole weekends, but his deftness in handling people and his almost infallible judgment as to what could or could not be profitably and usefully published made him a man to be greatly admired and respected.

I also met various members of the Macmillan organisation who had done so much to popularise my books for the past six years, and Dr. Eugene Nida, of the American bible society.

Guy Brown proved a splendid host and took us to see the park at Bear Mountain, where we saw humming birds in their natural state for the first time. He also took us to America's top military academy, West Point, and showed us some magnificent scenery. And we were treated to the usual trip by boat round Manhattan Island. Had it not been for the oppressive heat we should have been thoroughly happy. In the evenings entertainment was laid on and we were taken to the world-renowned Radio City on one evening and on another to see "Tea-house of the August Moon". Theatres and restaurants were all air-conditioned, and so was our room at the hotel, but to walk through the streets was like treading the floors of an oven. Two small things remain in my mind as first impressions. One is simply that amid a forest of skyscrapers the churches were at ground level. They looked, in their setting, like places of worship for dolls or fairies. I should have thought that some enterprising American would have built a church at the top of some skyscraper. Perhaps he has, by now. The other strong impression was the almost hysterical attitude towards the possibility of fire. To park your car by a fire-hydrant was to be guilty of a crime little less than murder.

The west coast

Early in the morning of August 20th we were driven by Guy Brown to La Guardia airport. Here we embarked on a four-engined propeller-driven plane destined for Los Angeles via Chicago. It was our first long-distance flight and as I have several times since travelled in modern high-speed jets I can see now why we found it such a long and tedious journey. The noise was thunderous and although we were air-conditioned we all got very weary from the noise and bumpiness of the flight. However we eventually touched down safely in Los Angeles and were met by our hosts, Walt James, Ralph Hamburger and Dick Halverson. I had not realised that L.A. airport was some distance from Hollywood and we were driven across a deadly flat plain dotted with "nodding donkeys" – small oil pumps perpetually sucking up the precious mineral from literally thousands of privately owned wells. This, I thought, is the side of Los Angeles we are never shown on the silver screen. The city itself was crowded and filled with the famous smog – a vaguely purple mist of stale exhaust fumes which made the eyes smart and stomachs uneasy.

We were housed by Walt (now Doctor) James, and he and his family were kindness itself to us. My first speaking engagement was at the First Hollywood Presbyterian church, but in the few intervening days a welcome party in the shape of an outdoor picnic was laid on for us, and we were introduced to all kinds of charming and interesting people. It was hot there, but never stiflingly so, and the evenings almost always brought a cool breeze and the endless chirruping of the cicadas. I had often heard this sound on American films before but had never known what it was.

On Sunday August 22nd, in a temperature of over 100° and wearing for courtesy's sake a Geneva gown, I preached three sermons, two in the morning and one in the evening. I was most kindly received and signed a good many autographs.

Forest Home conference centre
On the next day we set out for Forest Home conference centre, a beautiful place set 5,000 feet up on the wooded slopes of St. Bernardino mountain, some eighty miles east of Hollywood. I was not at all surprised to see a conspicuous sign at the entrance to the centre informing us that we were "one mile nearer Heaven"! What enthusiastic American Christian could resist that? Nevertheless in another sense it was a heavenly place with beautiful mountain scenery and, apart from the human beings, a sense of profound quiet.

I was asked to give an hour's lecture a day, for the first week to adults (mostly young marrieds) and in the second week to university students. I was a little disconcerted to find at least six microphones in front of me whenever I spoke. These were for private tape-recorders. The whole place was beautifully designed with dormitories and sleeping cabins, a spacious day lounge, a meeting hall, a bookshop and indeed every facility that one could wish for, including a swimming pool. This carried a warning notice that "swimmers should be careful – you cannot do at 5,000 feet what you can do at sea level". I was not tempted personally for although the sun was hot the water was icy cold, being formed from the melting snows of the mountain above us.

The days were spent in innumerable introductions and conversations, fairly exhausting in that heat but on the whole thoroughly rewarding. Although the Forest Home centre was owned by the Presbyterian Church (and frequently rented to other denominations throughout the year) the people I talked with were by no means all Presbyterian. A few were without any Church affiliation at all and when they (possibly through the preaching or lecturing of one of the speakers) decided to lead the Christian life there was the immediate and painful problem of deciding on the denomination to which they should be attached. I don't think I have ever felt the pain of our unhappy divisions so sharply before or since.

The driving force behind the whole campaign of putting the claims of Christ before the people of today was a remarkable woman, Henrietta Mears. She died some years ago, but she was an intelligent and deeply spiritual leader. Apart from the Presbyterian helpers I remember a Methodist minister and one Anglican priest besides myself. We used to meet for prayer daily, and in a flash I found myself back in Cambridge C.U. days, trying my best to pray with someone who was praying aloud, fluently and extempore. The trouble with extempore prayer is that one requires more than normal mental agility to understand the thoughts of the pray-er, and to turn those thoughts into prayer of any real significance. I think the best way for a group to pray together is for one to lead and suggest subjects and that each subject is followed by silence. This gives time for concentration, and one is not harassed by a continuous flow of words. Nevertheless I would not for one moment question the sincerity and fervour of those with whom I prayed at Forest Home.

We were most comfortably accommodated. The food was excellent but, by our standards, overwhelming in quantity. The days were strenuous for, apart from the countless

131

conversations, reporters from local papers dropped in fairly frequently and wanted to know my views on this and that. I tried to be careful for I was at that time and in that place a V.I.P., and it would have been only too easy to have been quoted as the voice of Britain.

I had had no experience in my own country of being regarded as an eminent man, and the general friendliness and admiration I was given by these Americans was good, perhaps too good, for the *ego*. I think it can certainly be said that I was greatly supported by the enthusiasm of the crowds. When I mentally compared the general apathy I had met at home with this sincere desire to idolise me, I was wryly amused. One couple said to me, "You know, Doctor Phillips, we've driven 200 miles to hear you speak." I couldn't help replying, "Well, thank you, but where I come from there are thousands who wouldn't even cross the road to do that."

Another Sunday of preaching three times at Hollywood Presbyterian church followed. Just before the second of the two morning services I was told, quite casually, that this service was to be televised. As far as I was concerned this meant little more than some extra, and rather hot lights.

The second week of my lecturing was to undergraduates and graduates of both sexes, and there were, according to the local press, some 500 of them present. As I entered the hall on the first morning I was greeted by the first, and possibly the last, standing ovation to come my way. It is a most moving experience. And that was not all. I was at all times listened to with the deepest attention, and afterwards was questioned with the greatest interest and by some with deep intellectual curiosity. After a day or two I was asked to speak for longer than the fifty-five minutes I usually aimed at. "Well, how long?" I asked simply. "As long as you like," they replied. So on the next morning I went on talking for an hour and fifty minutes. I think this was my record, though I frequently exceeded the hour.

E.S.P. again

It might be interesting here to mention an incident which once more suggested that I had, very occasionally, extra-sensory powers. The occasion was that Margery, my secretary, always a little accident-prone, bless her, had slipped on the pathway as she dashed to run an errand for me, and had knocked herself out by striking her head on the concrete. She was unconscious for a while and it was thought wise to send for an ambulance to take her to the hospital in Redlands, the nearest sizable town. A radio call was sent and acknowledged, but it seemed a long time before help came. My wife volunteered to accompany Margery in the ambulance and another car followed to bring her back. The time was after 8 p.m. and my wife recalls a nightmarish journey down the mountain roads, for the ambulance radio was going full blast receiving calls and repeat calls all the way down.

Shortly before 11 p.m. I began to get anxious. Surely my wife should be back by now. Or had Margery's injury proved worse than we thought, and had she felt she ought to stay on in the hospital. I knelt by my bed and as far as I could I put my anxieties in the hands of God. As I got up from my knees I heard the sound of a car approaching, its tyres shuffling on the soft sandy road. I looked at my watch and saw that it was 11.04 p.m. I heard my wife's voice say, "Thank you very much for the lift. Good night." Then a man's voice said, "Good night," and I heard the car drive away. I went outside expecting to see her there but there was no one there at all. I then experienced a strange sense of peace, flung myself down on the bed and fell immediately asleep. Exactly one hour later, at 12.04 a.m., I heard the car again with the same shuffling noise of tyres on soft sand. The car stopped, my wife got out and said the same words as I had heard her speak before. But this time I was actually present, for I had dashed from my bed as soon as I heard the noise of the car approaching. My emotions were confused but I was overwhelmingly glad to see my wife safely back, and to learn that Margery was only slightly concussed. But what had happened? Was this a genuine case of precognition or merely my vivid imagination? I cannot answer that except to say that what I have set down happened just like that.

Santa Barbara

Americans are very generous but they certainly work you hard. How often have I heard such a comment from some speaker or writer who has been persuaded to go on a lecture tour. Their generosity appeared in all kinds of ways, some unexpected. For instance they gave me some clothes (very lightweight and more suitable for the climate) and a personal love-gift of a hundred dollars. With the utmost friendliness and tact they urged me never to mention my salary as an Anglican vicar. "You see," they explained a little shame-facedly, "many Americans rate a man entirely by what he earns, and some of our ministers earn five or six times your salary."

Nevertheless, although they provided me with adequate dollars, free hospitality and travel facilities I felt they were determined to get the most out of me while I was there.

One day I was asked to address a holiday club in Santa Barbara, about 150 miles away, of which the members were all divorced men and women. Since time was short it was suggested that I should be flown there in a light two-seater plane. Now I love flying, but I have never felt so small and insignificant. On our right was the massive mountain range which houses the giant telescope of Mount Palomar. At 10,000 feet or so we seemed a mere nothing flying in an empty sky over a pitiless desert. The noise was considerable and I grew hotter and hotter. Conversation was impossible but I managed to convey my discomfort to the young pilot. He merely grinned and pointed to the *outside* temperature gauge mounted in the perspex canopy. This indicated that outside the tiny plane the air was just below freezing point.

Over his shoulder I studied the instrument panel as best I could, and as we came into land I noticed a little green light mounted below the words, "Landing gear DOWN." As we came down this light did not come on, and I wondered how I could communicate this fact to the pilot without distracting him. Finally I decided to keep quiet. The young man had had several years of flying experience and was, moreover, the son of the chairman of the company who built the plane. We landed safely and smoothly and as soon as we had clambered out I mentioned my fears to him. "Oh, no problem," he replied with a cheerful grin, "she would have made a perfect belly landing without the wheels anyhow."

The Christian holiday club in Santa Barbara was arranged in and around a truly splendid old Spanish mansion with the most lovely furnishings imaginable. I have never found a more delightful audience and I was afterwards charmed by the impeccable manners and general good humour of those to whom I talked. It seemed incredible to me that all these attractive men and delightful women were *divorced*. It also seemed very strange indeed that a Christian Church should organise a special holiday retreat entirely for the divorced. And yet, why not?

I deliberately avoided the party late that night. I had another strenuous Sunday ahead of me, and felt that an early bed was called for. I was no sooner in bed than three of the Presbyterian ministers called in to see that I was all right, and to make arrangements for transport in the morning.

Lake Tahoe

Well I survived that Sunday too, and early on Monday morning we set out in a large car for a 550-mile journey to the other holiday centre at which I was booked to speak. This was on the shores of Lake Tahoe, a really beautiful place on the Nevada border. The first 150 miles was over the most horrifying desert I had ever seen, utterly flat and featureless, with no living thing in sight. It was the Mojave desert. I was not surprised to learn that no one was allowed to travel on that road without carrying ten extra gallons of water.

The pattern of the week's conference at Lake Tahoe was much the same as that we had followed at Forest Home. This meant for me a daily lecture, attending discussions and being available for counselling. It was called a family conference, which meant in fact that we met many delightful young couples with children. I don't think that the conference aimed at converting the pagan, so much as strengthening the faith of those who were already Christians. Quite apart from the value of any good counsel which we, the speakers and leaders might give, there is a definite value in the getting together of young Christians, temporarily cut off from the distractions of a largely pagan culture. I am pretty certain that they returned to their normal lives strengthened and refreshed.

At the end of the week we were motored back to Sacramento by the Reverend Robert Ferguson. I was due to speak three times at his church, the Freemont Presbyterian church. I must confess that by this time I was getting really tired of *speaking*, even though my material could be repeated several times to different audiences. I was therefore very glad to hear that we were to go back to Hollywood, to stay once more with the Walt Jameses and see a little of the ordinary life of that very unusual part of the world. We were driven to San Francisco airport, and wished we had more time to explore that fascinating city. We left by an evening plane for Hollywood's Burbank airport. A perfect sunset lay behind us and it was certainly one of the most delightful and relaxing flights I have ever made. At one point, as darkness fell, I was a little alarmed to see that the rear end of each of the four engines was glowing a dull red. However I was assured that this was perfectly normal, and it was simply because I had not previously flown by night that I had not noticed the phenomenon.

Return visit to Hollywood

Once back in Hollywood I, at any rate, attempted to unwind. Walt and his wife Marguerite were the most considerate of hosts, leaving us alone when we wanted above all to rest; at other times ready to drive us anywhere we wished. One evening we were taken to the mountain-top above Los Angeles and looked down on the sparkling farflung lights of that city. But even this lovely sight was blurred by the ever-present noxious smog. One day we braved this unpleasant atmosphere and drove down to do a little shopping. The price of almost everything was staggeringly high, and we noticed how highly valued, and highly priced, were English goods.

I was also struck by some Los Angeles slum property, haunted by pathetic-looking "poor whites". The degree of decay and squalor was worse than any that I have seen in London or any other British city. Yet within a few miles were the magnificent homes of Hollywood's rich, all equipped with swimming pools and perpetually watered lawns.

We had dinner with the minister of the Hollywood Presbyterian church, the Reverend Louis H. Evans, an urbane and charming host. Strangely enough what I remember most of that visit was having coffee on the patio, after dinner, and the fact that there were growing, quite naturally, and bearing fruit, lemon trees.

We also enjoyed a meal with that dynamic personality Henrietta Mears, in her luxurious house. She thought, and possibly she was right in the hot-house atmosphere of Hollywood, that the only way to make contact with the rich was to live in their own luxurious style. Certainly she met many influential, and wealthy, people and, knowing her, I have no doubt that she used every opportunity to put over to them the claims of Christ.

We were driven to the Hollywood Bowl, surely a magnificent auditorium by any standards. We were also driven around to see and admire the lovely houses and estates of various film stars. It was hard to realise that the whole of the Los Angeles district would have been nothing but desert but for the enormous dams which had been built up in the mountains on the eastward side. Rain rarely falls at any time of the year and there is almost unvarying sunshine. It is easy to see how the film industry came to settle in a place with a climate ideal for its purposes. We realised this particularly when, on my birthday in mid-September, we paid a visit to Paramount Studios. All the paraphernalia of film-making from stage coaches to mountain sets were just lying about in the sun since shelter from wind and rain was scarcely necessary. It was all rather disillusioning. The sheriff's office was apparently there, but once the door was opened there was nothing inside – all interior shots being made in a studio. Shop fronts, the exteriors of western hotels or livery stables were all there, but since they were all merely exterior shells there was a ghost-town appearance to almost everything.

There was one particular set, made indoors in a vast hangar-like studio. It was made to appear like a luxurious garden, complete with swimming pool. Our daughter, a keen swimmer, ran across to the pool only to discover there was no water in it, indeed only one side which the cameras would see was in any way finished. Then we discovered that the lawn was made of plastic grass, that all the flowers were similarly manmade, and that even the trees were cunningly built up with artificial leaves and branches. This was disillusionment enough, but in a few minutes we were asked to see an actual shot. The scene was the interior of an aeroplane and the sole action was the handing down of a blanket from the rack by the air hostess to cover the knees of a passenger. There were perhaps two lines of dialogue, but this particular shot was made twelve times. Personally I could not see the remotest difference between any of the brief performances. I remember Jennifer's disgust with the fact that the plane had no wings. It was difficult to explain that since wings would not be seen by the cameras, there was no necessity to build them. My wife and I were particularly impressed by the almost military discipline shown on all hands. Whatever men, or women, were doing – painting, sawing, even hammering in nails – everything stopped at once the moment the clapper-board snapped shut for a take. Similarly, once the shot was over and the cameras commanded to cut, the work began again instantly.

We met some very delightful people at Paramount. I had a forty-minute chat with Cecil B. de Mille, who was preparing *The Ten Commandments*. I was astonished to see his almost obsessional demand for accuracy and detail. Where one would have thought that plastic or even papier mâché would have sufficed he insisted that heathen gods and goddesses should be really carved, from stone, by stonemasons. I never saw the film but I was much impressed by de Mille's enthusiasm over the whole project.

We met James Stewart, a quiet impressive man, and were told that he was churchwarden at his own Episcopal church. We also met the intelligent and charming Joan Davis. But the special guest, whom we did not really expect to see, was the one I had asked for as a birthday treat, to wit, Danny Kaye. In old working jeans he suddenly appeared at our luncheon table, and a delightful, though surprisingly quiet, guest he proved to be. It was obvious that he could switch off his clowning, his humour or his pathos, at will. Thus, as he was not at that moment working, he was just a quiet highly intelligent human being who made a charming companion.

New York and home

So, after a few days' most hospitable treatment, we left Los Angeles to fly to New York. This time, with the benefit of a ninety-mile-an-hour tail wind, the journey was made in ten and a half hours, including a stop at Kansas City. Once again Macmillans had booked hotel accommodation for us in New York, ready for embarkation on the *Ile de France* next morning.

Perhaps the less I say about the journey back the better. We missed the high standards of Cunard, and it was disappointing to find, for example, that a cigarette dropped on the first day of the voyage was still there on the last. The food was adequate but poor in taste and variety compared with the fare we had enjoyed on the *Queen Elizabeth*. Worst of all was the difficulty, if not the impossibility, of getting a bath. It seemed to us passengers that the French thought five days not an unreasonable time to do without.

The *Ile de France* had an uncomfortable motion in anything like a rough sea, and we were all extremely glad to be put off by tender at Plymouth. Never had England appeared so green and pleasant. Within a few hours we were back in Redhill, Surrey.

Farewell to St. John's

I had promised to give St. John's, Redhill, ten years of my life, and that meant only just over three months to tidy up personal affairs and to see that the parish was in as good working order as I could make it for my successor. I knew that Pat Simpson and Norman Mantle would stay on for the present and so that was no particular worry. I told them of my proposed departure and then I broke it to my churchwardens. Soon afterwards I had to tell the parish at large of my plans, and I must confess I was a little surprised by the many expressions of regret.

Although I have complained of the deadly apathy of the

parish of St. John's, I do not in any way mean to criticise the group of faithful people who supported me and my colleagues in all kinds of ways. There was no apathy there, and I found enthusiasm and generosity of both time and money from quite a number of men and women. Rather to my surprise, eight men came forward for ordination either during or soon after my time as vicar. I am still surprised for I certainly never urged the career of an ordained man on anyone. Still, if these decisions were in some sort a result of my own ministry I am truly thankful.

My wife and I will always be grateful to the parochial church council for their personal kindness. I was also lucky enough to have the secretarial services of our invaluable verger, Margery. How few vicars have a first-class shorthand typist available for the not inconsiderable correspondence and general paperwork that is the lot of every Anglican vicar?

Looking back at those ten years at Redhill my chief impression is one of enormous busy-ness. True, I "rejoiced in my strength" and did not really mind working hard and long. Nevertheless I am still well aware of a great many things I did not have time to do, and, naturally, of a good many things I might have done more thoroughly.

My farewell letter in the parish magazine concluded:

I shall not lightly forget my ten years at St. John's. In many ways it has been very uphill work, but this I think was inevitable since the years following the war were probably difficult in any parish. Now, however, I can with a clear conscience hand on to Sidney Dyer a "going concern", a church which is paying its way, which has a spiritual nucleus and a good many supporters of various kinds. What is more, there is every evidence that the best is yet to be, and that future years will bring to fruition several things which are at present hardly more than germinating. Please do not forget to pray for your church.

10

Attitudes to the New Testament

The New Testament in the original Greek is not a work of literary art; it is not written in a solemn ecclesiastical language, it is written in the sort of Greek which was spoken over the Eastern Mediterranean after Greek had become an international language and therefore lost its real beauty and subtlety. In it we see Greek used by people who have no real feeling for Greek words because Greek words are not the words they spoke when they were children. It is a sort of "basic" Greek; a language without roots in the soil, a utilitarian, commercial and administrative language (C. S. Lewis, from his introduction to *Letters to Young Churches*)

Translation Aims
The language used must be that commonly spoken;
the translation should expand if necessary to preserve the original meaning;
the letters should read like letters, not theological treatises;
the translation should flow;
the value of the version should lie in its easy-to-read quality.
(J. B. Phillips on the translation of *Letters to Young Churches*)

Method of translation
Perhaps it might be of interest at this point to outline my method of translation. It sounds simple enough, but it is somewhat fatiguing, and, since I loathe repetitive tasks of any kind, it can prove irksome. But the final result must naturally not show any of the mental conflicts and difficulties in making ultimate decisions.

The first thing to do is to empty the mind of the only too familiar Authorised Version. This proved, in the event, not nearly as difficult as I had feared. For one thing, although no one has a higher opinion of the A.V. as literature than I, it is undoubtedly old-fashioned. Further, it is written from Genesis to Revelation in a consistently beautiful English style. Absolutely no concession is made to the differing characteristics of the writers, whether of the Old or New Testaments. Of course I understand the motives of the translators of the 1611 version. Here before them was the very Word of God and it must be rendered into the finest possible English. For the same reasons which made the monks illuminate, with rare care and skill, portions of scripture, and for the same reasons which made them represent the ugly cross, a roadside gibbet, as a thing of beauty, often made of precious metal and richly jewelled, the Bible itself was made into an English literary masterpiece. Now, frankly it isn't. Certainly the Bible contains much rich poetry and sublimely economical narrative, certainly it gives us truths which no man could guess at or find in any other way, but its general style is uneven, dependent on the abilities of the writers themselves, moved, as I believe they were, by the Holy Spirit.

Thus having trained myself to understand the ordinary communicative English of today I had only to immerse myself in the Greek and effect the transition. At no time was I bothered by recollections of the Authorised Version. My task demanded too much concentration for that. I am blessed, or perhaps cursed, with a vivid imagination and as I tried to understand as fully as possible what the original authors were saying in Greek, I began to feel myself in person as Paul or Mark or Luke or John.

Having cleared the mind thoroughly the next step was to read the Greek, first quickly in order to get the drift or drive as well as the flavour of a certain passage. Then I would read it slowly, looking out for any unusual construction of words or indeed any unusual New Testament word. Until 1972, when I made my final revision, I did not refer to anyone else's translation, but I did look up in a commentary a word or phrase which puzzled me.

The ground work then was to make an accurate, but not polished, translation of the Greek into modern English. Then

142

I forgot about the Greek and attempted to shape the English for modern ears. This was a matter of reading to myself, or reading to my wife or my secretary, and sometimes asking them to read it back to me. At times a whole passage was put away for weeks till our combined critical faculties were back to normal. Sometimes after this interval I was astonished that I had passed a horrible piece of translator's jargon, and felt bound to try again. Sometimes I imagined myself to be the reader rather than the writer of the documents. I tried to be a member of the Ephesian or Philippian church (only under-standing modern English) or I tried to feel like Timothy or Titus. Feeble as these efforts may have been, I think they account for a certain personal feeling which some critics have discerned.

The final, and sometimes humiliating, part of the process was to compare my modern English with what the Greek said. It was sometimes humiliating because in the course of mod-ernising a passage I had missed out some vital ingredient or flavour which the Greek undoubtedly possessed. It is a fasci-nating task, but it is undeniably hard work. It is also a very lonely task; my wife could, and did, help me with modern English but she knows very little Greek. When I was really in difficulty I used to approach an old friend and contemporary, Charlie Moule, Lady Margaret Professor of Divinity at Cam-bridge, in my view easily the ablest scholar in N.T. Greek in England today. I would sometimes say, hopefully, "Could this phrase possibly mean this?" And he, the gentlest of men but a scholar of the highest integrity, would say firmly and politely "No".

A controversial verse

One little twist which I gave in my translation caused me scores of letters and was really not worth the bother. This was in my rendering of Romans 8:32. In the Authorised Version of 1611 this reads: "He that spared not his own Son, but deli-vered him up for us all etc." The trouble lies in the word "spare". To use it in the sense of "shield" seemed to me to be on the decline in modern English, while to use it in the sense of "give" seemed to me quite strong and up-to-date. I therefore at one point made the passage read, "He that did not hesitate to spare his own Son etc." My purpose in this innocent twist was simply a shock device to break through a familiar passage containing a not very well used word and present God's incredible generosity afresh.

It soon became evident that many people did not know that spare meant more than one thing. We probably all recognise one difference at least; that shown in the common sayings, "Spare the rod and spoil the child," and "Please spare a penny for the old man's hat." In the first the meaning is, "don't use" and in the second "give". But Webster's Dictionary gives no less than six different meanings to the word, with several sub-divisions. (The six are, for the reader's interest: (a) "to refrain from punishing or to show mercy to" (b) "to refrain from attacking" (physically or verbally) (c) "to relieve some-one of the necessity of doing" (d) "to refrain from" = to avoid (e) "to use frugally or stintingly" (f) "to give up or part with as not being strictly needed". And there are many more subsidiary meanings.

It is obvious that the Authorised Version is using sense "a", while I was using sense "f". I could justify my use of the English word, but it does not really reflect the Greek word *pheidomai*. So, in the end and after what seemed innumerable letters, I hauled down my private flag and revised my version to, "He who did not grudge his Son but gave him up for us all etc". This is perhaps a bit of a compromise, but it avoids the use of the word spare which has become largely colourless, and which most of us do not use as much as once a year.

The fundamentalist view

As might be expected I met with a series of (mostly friendly) letters from fundamentalists, chiefly in the U.S.A. Many of them were very dubious about my "soundness in the faith", and told me so very plainly. After writing scores of patient letters over the years I composed a form letter of which I still keep copies and one of these is sent automatically to any fire-breathing fundamentalist.

I was not brought up with any fundamentalist views of the Bible, although the utmost reverence was always accorded to

Holy Writ. I did not meet fundamentalism until my Cambridge days, when this "cover-to-cover dictated by God" view was an essential part of Christian Union faith and fellowship. For some years, with some inner reservations, I held this view and it was naturally nourished by the good-hearted but not over-bright Father Trout. I think it was after my first curacy in Penge, and during many months of thought during and after convalescing that I allowed my mind to open up. It had previously seemed to me that on the one hand lay certainty, definite and uncompromising, and anywhere else lay doubt, uncertainty and a frightening responsibility of choice. Happily, little by little, I began to meet others who were not strictly fundamentalist; I attended churches which were not rigidly Protestant evangelical, and, perhaps above all, I began to read far more widely than ever. I had never had much sympathy for the Catholic point of view, and indeed I have little today; it is not for me. But I read quite a lot of Catholic, modernist and liberal books and began to feel considerably liberated. I retained (and still retain) my enormous reverence for, and delight in, the N.T., but my reasons for this attitude were now different. It was no longer blind faith informed by reason which supported me. There was no longer any niggling doubt that one blast of honest commonsense could disintegrate a shaky structure at any moment. Now, and of course the feeling grew with the years, I felt confident that no one could damage a faith which had endured my own fiercely critical attacks. Today, forty odd years later, despite my own temperamental fears and doubts, I am intellectually utterly sure of the God revealed, however partially and incompletely, in the N.T.

A caution to fundamentalists

Today I can write with honesty and in kindness to the most perfervid fundamentalist, and tell him that though I believe in the Christian fundamental implicitly, I could not hold the fundamentalist view of the Bible. I ask him to consider the following indisputable facts:

(a) In no case do we possess the original document of any N.T. book.

145

(b) God has not dictated the Bible in the English of the seventeenth century for all men, for all time.

(c) The 1611 version is not the literal translation he supposes. For example, Matthew 27:44 is translated "the thieves also which were crucified with him, *cast the same in his teeth.*" Now these words are fine, vivid and memorable, but not one of those in italics appears in the Greek, which simply says, *oneidizon*, which means "abused" or "kept on abusing" him. And of course there are many other, though less striking examples.

(d) The language used, particularly the picture language, is tied to a particular Oriental country of nearly two thousand years ago. This is the land of vines and fig trees, of corn and wine, houses and cattle – all of which are probably meaningless to, shall we say, the Eskimo, for whom Christ also died. And you cannot talk meaningfully about a ship or an anchor to a people who have never even seen navigable water.

(e) There are some 1750 known human languages and the literal translation into many of them is impossible, often simply because no equivalent word *exists* in those languages. The splendid army of translators use the utmost ingenuity to convey *meaning*, but literal translation is frequently impossible.

(f) Many languages lack a word for "love" in the Christian sense. Again and again what Christians regard as key words of their faith have no direct equivalent, and the hard-pressed translator is driven to circumlocution to convey his meaning.

(g) Jesus spoke in Aramaic, which is a popular form of Hebrew. It is possible, of course, that he knew Greek, but it would have been of little purpose to preach or teach in that language to a people who heard Hebrew every Sabbath and spoke Aramaic every day, but knew no other language. Yet the gospels are set down in a workaday Greek commonly spoken and written throughout the enormous Empire of Rome. We cannot therefore know exactly what Jesus said on most occasions. The only exceptions are when Mark, whose gospel was based on Peter's reminiscences, sometimes gives the actual Aramaic words which Jesus used.

(h) This "cover-to-cover" inspiration idea is of comparative recent growth, and is probably not more than 200 years old. The great Protestant reformer Martin Luther certainly had no fundamentalist views, and referred to James' letter as a "right strawy epistle" though he later somewhat modified his views. No, what happened from the earliest days was that the body of believers, the Church, chose, cherished and highly reverenced the early writings which had survived. They debated long and earnestly and they rejected quite a lot of material. (Incidentally, the second letter of Peter only got included in the sacred list by the skin of its teeth – and some say it didn't deserve to.)

Inspiration

What then are we to make of this diverse collection of small books, from Matthew to Revelation? Can we regard them as uniquely inspired and therefore authoritative? I think we can, but a little honest thought must be exercised.

First let us look at history. In the year 56 a man by the name of Paul wrote a letter to a group of people living in Corinth, a Greek city, seaport and commercial centre. Corinth was, like many ports, full of vice and violence, but it was worse than this. It had become a by-word in the ancient world for sexual corruption, drink and drugs, crooked dealing, and every kind of knavery. It could well cater for all the depraved and perverted instincts of man. The Greeks, as usual, had a word for it *korinthiazesthai*, and to "go through the Corinth experience", which the word means, meant a thorough plunge into all the pleasures and excitements, all the vices and corruptions which the world could afford. To this notorious city Paul wrote these words: "Don't be under any illusion – neither the impure, the idolator or the adulterer; neither the effeminate the pervert or the thief; neither the swindler, the drunkard, the foul-mouthed or the rapacious shall have any share in the kingdom of God."

And then he added, "and such were some of you" (1 Cor. 6:11). I think that this single sentence is one of the most important ever written. Nobody doubts the existence and authenticity of this letter. But who can explain it, except by admitting that some new force of character-changing capacity

147

has come into the human scene? In all the New Testament letters this strange supernatural force is recognised, reckoned upon or expected, by writers of such diverse temperaments as Paul, Peter and James. All of these men, writing in and to an almost wholly pagan environment, connect this new power in human living with a man Jesus, publicly executed a few years before they wrote their letters and now plainly alive and operative in many hundreds of human beings.

Naturally we are led on to see what sort of person this Jesus was, and we find ten years and more later four brief and, in some ways, widely divergent, accounts of his life and teaching. And we read also of the subsequent impact of that life on human contemporary history – of how a small and previously disheartened and discouraged band of followers set out as a spearhead of nothing less than the transformation of the world.

In face of such a mass of indisputable historic evidence I really cannot understand any unprejudiced mind being anything other than deeply impressed. And when the same sort of character transformation is observed today, not once but hundreds of times, who could fail to be deeply moved? I tried with all the concentration I could muster to *detach* myself from these artless but profound first century manuscripts, but it was utterly impossible. Certainly you can detach yourself from linguistic style, though that is hard work enough, but there is no escape or insulation from the throbbing insistence of the voice of God. After hundreds of hours of the most careful concentration of which I am capable, I could not avoid being challenged, frightened, exhilarated and stimulated by words twenty centuries old. The eternal resonance breaks through, and, being human, we cannot avoid sympathetic vibration in the deepest recesses of our hearts.

Two witnesses

Two particularly striking examples of the present-day power of the N.T. came to me. One elegantly written and beautifully expressed letter in English came from a seventy-seven-year-old Japanese business man. He commuted daily from his home to his work in Tokyo, and if we have ever seen on television the incredible crowding that this commuting entails we may wonder even more at the story. Apparently during his daily journeys my Japanese friend had, over the months, read *Letters to Young Churches*. He wrote to me, with a joy that was instantly communicated, how "for the first time he had understood what Christianity was all about, and that his whole life was transformed". Not many people are transformed at the age of seventy-seven, and I was immensely touched not only by the extraordinary evidence of God's power working through the written word but by the grace and courtesy of this charming old man who took the trouble to sit down and write such words of gratitude and dignified exuberance to me.

The other particularly memorable letter came from New Zealand. A young man, who was continually in trouble with the police, was eventually sentenced to a term in reformatory school. He did not respond but rebelled violently against all rules and discipline. Eventually he was condemned to a period of "solitary". According to the rules he was allowed to take two books with him, one scientific and one religious. For the latter he chose *Letters to Young Churches*. Once more, as in Corinth nearly 2,000 years ago, the miracle happened. The young man was completely changed. After serving his term alone he wrote to his former headmaster, to his old school magazine, and no doubt to many others, telling simply what had happened. "Old things had passed away – all things had become new," as the New Testament says. I heard all this through the young man's headmaster, and I was very deeply moved. How can anyone deny the power of God speaking without human intermediary through his inspired writings?

Evidence

I began to receive, in an ever increasing flood, thousands of letters from almost all over the English-speaking world. Men and women, some old and some middle-aged, sent me a constant stream of thankful letters. This current went on for over twenty years and still breaks out in new springs and rivulets. Every letter was answered and I have numbers of packed files which in themselves are a formidable body of evidence for the Christian faith which cannot surely be lightly ignored. I should be very surprised if the studies of our modern clever-clevers, who know so much better about New Testament events than the men who witnessed them, and who have done so much to whittle down and even destroy the faith of thousands, show much evidence of this kind.

I tell my tale simply, no doubt to some minds naively. But I hope it will be crystal clear how I felt bound to abandon the "God-dictated-every-word-from-cover-to-cover" attitude, and won an attitude which commends itself to my intelligence as well as my faith, and corresponds with my deepest experience. And I think that the most dyed-in-the-wool fundamentalist will see, if he thinks carefully, that he can count me as an ally over Christian fundamentals.

A matter of communication

The work of the translator is, as I see it, to convey the meaning of one language into the meaning and sense of another. He cannot help being an interpreter although, if he is a conscientious man, he will not allow his personal feelings to colour his interpretations. He is somewhat in the position of an interpreter between the heads of state at an international conference. His sole work is to convey, as accurately as he can, comments or views expressed in one language into another language altogether. However competent he is, his work can never be completely perfect. For not only do the words of one country contain overtones and shades of meaning which are not matched in the words of the other country, but the whole cultural and ethical background of the two countries may be so widely dissimilar that accurate communication is a work of genius. This illustration may serve to show how daunting is the work of the modern translator of the New Testament. The message he is required to transmit is, he believes, both universal and eternal. Yet the more he studies sympathetically the world of the young Church as well as his contemporary world, the more he feels in despair at making accurate translation. Patterns of thought, the extent of human knowledge, and even ways of everyday living were so different 2,000 years ago that to attempt to reproduce them conscien-

150

tiously in modern English could easily result in making the Gospel seem more than ever far away and long ago.

But suppose he pursues a different and more helpful line? Suppose he remembers that human nature and basic human needs are the same in all centuries. Then he will aim not at one hundred per cent accuracy, which is impossible in any case, but at equivalent effect. That is to say, he will try to reproduce in today's hearers and readers the same emotions as were produced by the original documents so long ago. This, to my mind, is a very difficult, but not hopelessly impossible objective.

Translator's English

I have a collection of several hundreds of examples of translator's English which I have noted in recent years. It would be wearisome to point out the occasional infelicities to be found in Weymouth, Moffat and even that excellent American translator, Goodspeed. But Ronald Knox, who aimed at a style that should be timeless, produces the same sort of unhappiness in such a paragraph as this:

> Nobody can say that we are encroaching, that you lie beyond our orbit; our journeys in preaching Christ's gospel took us all the way to you. Ours, then, is no disproportionate boasting, founded on other men's labours; on the contrary, as your faith bears increase we hope to attain still further vantage points through you, without going beyond our province, and preach the gospel further afield, without boasting of ready-made conquests in a province that belongs to another. He who boasts should make his boast in the Lord; it is man whom God accredits, not the man who takes credit to himself, that proves himself to be true metal (2 Cor. 10:14–18).

There is no doubt about the meaning here, but what strange English is this? Again if we look into the careful scholarly work of E. V. Rieu we find such sentences as this:

"But one cannot break into the Strong One's house and plunder his goods unless one begins by tying up the Strong One. After that one will ransack his house" (Mark 3:27).

151

"To which Jesus replied: 'Consent now. It behoves us to conform with all right usage.' And John consented" (Matt. 3:15).

Living in two worlds

It would seem obvious that the successful translator must know very well indeed the languages of those for whom he is required to interpret. But strangely enough the New Testament scholar of today is considered perfectly adequate for the task if he has a thorough knowledge of Greek and its usages. Few seem to realise that it is every bit as essential that he should know the usage and thought-forms of his English-speaking contemporaries in various walks of life and in various parts of the English-speaking world. The scholar is all too often isolated from the workaday world; he is inclined to use a word or expression which is most beautifully apt in the ears of his fellow scholars, but which has long ago become an archaism to ordinary people. And when he does descend to the colloquial he is all too often inclined to use outdated slang.

For the moment I will only record my conviction that this knowledge of how ordinary people speak, write and think can only be acquired by reading all kinds of books and periodicals, and by honest conversation on friendly terms with people whose background is far from scholarly.

In recommending the use of ordinary English, I do not mean slang, or colloquial near-slang, which not only changes very rapidly, but varies greatly from place to place, and from country to country. I am suggesting as strongly as I can that there is a perfectly sound English vocabulary which is very widely used, quite outside intellectual circles.

I see, then, this problem of translation into modern English in terms of the thorough understanding both of the original Greek and of the vocabulary, thoughts and minds of the people who are likely to read in English today. But we must do even more than this. We have to use imaginative sympathy with the writers of long ago. We shall never get across the passionate urgency of Paul, for example, unless we use every scrap of knowledge and inference that we can find in order to put ourselves imaginatively in his shoes. Naturally, this is not easy, nor can it be done without its particular cost. But we must studiously avoid the sort of detachment which is sometimes adopted by the well bred English layman when he is asked to "read the lessons" in church. Quite possibly, on the technical level, he reads well, but if there is the faintest note of, "I am reading this as best I can, but it has nothing to do with me" in his diction, then he has no hope at all of communicating the real New Testament.

If we are to be successful translators we cannot afford to be detached. We must feel to the full the love and compassion, the near despair and the unshakable hope, the gay courage and the bitter hostility of this most extraordinary short period of human history. Unless we too experience the awe and wonder of the earlier disciples, unless we can share to some extent the certainty and fortitude of the young Church, and unless we can sympathise with the deep pastoral concern of the apostles, we shall never communicate the living heart of the New Testament writings, however immaculate our translation may be.

11

Happiness and Success in Swanage
1955

And so, apart from family contentment, here I was with the sea less than 400 yards away, the most delectable countryside all around us, owning my own house and garden and possessed of the most golden prospects, how could I fail to be happy? Christmas came with almost unbearable joy and I well remember helping a local vicar, Bill (now Canon) Langdon (who has become a close and valued friend) at his midnight communion. His church was just over a mile from here, "up the hill" at Langton Matravers. The joy of Christmas, the simple beauty of a village church, the thankfulness for a year of intense happiness filled me with inexpressible delight.

Settling into Swanage

The time is January, 1955, and the place Swanage, in England's lovely Dorset. Of course, as I might have known, despite many promises and reassurances, the house was not finished. For over a month Vera, Jennifer and I (and of course Margery) stayed at the comfortable and charming Wolfeton Hotel (now alas, demolished). In staying here we were not more than a few hundred yards from the house-building site, and could watch progress and visit it as often as we wished. The translational work continued with the enthusiastic high pressure which the work itself produced. In lounge or games room, indeed in any quiet corner of the Wolfeton, day after day I wrestled pleasurably enough, with Luke and his "Acts of the Apostles". Now that the vast burden of a large parish was lifted from my shoulders my energy seemed to be limitless. Not now for one morning a week, but every day, I was free to concentrate on a task which I loved. Letters, of course, continued to be forwarded. But they were far less of a burden now, set free as I was from a hundred time-consuming tasks. For a little while there were not even invitations to speak, for few people knew where I was.

It was a delightful time. After the rigours of winter in Redhill it was astonishing to find, a mere 120 miles away, an utterly different climate. Wind, even very violent wind, often blew but everything from the sea to charming Dorset country-side was clean and unspoiled. Even in January the brilliant sun (which seemed to me to shine a great deal in early 1955) was *hot*. All the beauty spots were naturally deserted at this time of the year, and apart from working hard at congenial work, we felt life was almost a perpetual holiday.

We found a very good little school for Jennifer (now eight and a half). It was called Toronto, and the extremely able head was a Miss Trotter. The school has now been converted into yet one more hotel, and at the time of writing Miss Trotter lives in quiet retirement. There can be no doubt that she continued to lay excellent foundations for our daughter's education.

I began to help in local churches at holy-communion and to preach in various pulpits. I was made very welcome every-where – indeed I think I was spoilt. For the time being my responsibilities were very small and, insofar as I thought much about it at all, I enjoyed making public appearances. What had often been an obligatory chore became a delight to be enjoyed when and where I chose.

Meanwhile, whenever it could be managed, we had to choose curtains and carpets and all the paraphernalia neces-sary for the furnishing of the new house. Bournemouth, some nine miles away, had excellent shops and we spent many happy hours picking, choosing and finally ordering. Fortu-nately, although Vera and I are so different in temperament, our artistic tastes are very similar. I do not normally enjoy shopping, but this was very different. This exercise was planned to embellish or beautify the first house we had ever owned. For fifteen years we had lived simply, though we were conscious of no lack and we never envied our richer friends. But now we had the prospect of more money than we ever dreamt of and we felt almost guilty as we chose what we wanted and were nearly always able to choose the best. This sounds as if we were preparing to live in a luxurious palace, but I am sure no one who visits us ever gets that impression. The house is built in the local Purbeck stone, but it is quite a small and conventional four-bedroomed detached house.

We moved in in February. It was immediately *home*, and all three of us were happy and immensely thankful and content. Margery had found comfortable digs quite close by, and made herself snug in her own room. We decided to make one of the bedrooms upstairs into my library-cum-study and for some months this worked well enough. But slowly the problems of noise began to be intolerable. The room was just above the kitchen and the noise of washing machine, electric polisher and a hundred and one smaller domestic noises made concentration very difficult at times. Conversely it was far from pleasant for Vera to endure the hours'-long barrage of a rather noisy typewriter. Eventually we solved this problem by a little extra building.

The Dorking mission

Before I had left Redhill I had been invited by the vicar of Dorking (Kenneth Evans, later Bishop of Dorking) to take part in the Guildford diocesan mission which was due to be held in 1956. I was much honoured and flattered to be thus chosen. It seemed to me to be a good idea to meet the clergy and most interested laymen a year beforehand to set out and discuss my ideas of what a mission should be. I am no Billy Graham, and my intentions were simple. I aimed to set forth on each weekday evening of the mission the basic facts of the Christian faith expressed in modern terms. I should appeal to the reason and commonsense of ordinary people. If emotion came into it it was never deliberately induced. My good friends at Dorking were most welcoming and kind and there was much lively discussion but no sort of disagreement. We were plainly of one mind and after a longish meeting and a plea for continued prayer I returned to Swanage.

Jock Gibb

Somewhere about this time (spring 1955) I have a note of "lunch with Jock Gibb". Jocelyn Gibb had, on the retirement of Geoffrey Bles in 1954, become the head of the firm and we became friends at once. I received nothing but kindness and understanding from Jock during the twenty years of our working together. He had great abilities and knew a lot about typeface, the proper quality of paper, and the ever-increasing prices of almost everything to do with printing and publishing. He has come down to Swanage several times and I have visited him on his Sussex farm. Many times have we gratefully received from him gifts of farm produce and every Christmas until his retirement I was sent a splendidly bound copy of my latest book, gleaming with the gloss of beautiful leather and the sparkle of gold lettering on its spine.

The reason for this particular lunch was, I am pretty sure, the forthcoming publication of *The Young Church in Action* – the title I had chosen for my translation of the Acts. We lunched at Jock's club, the Athenaeum, and he was surprised and delighted to hear of my rapid progress. The simple truth was no more than that I had very few other responsibilities and could work hard and fast almost continuously.

Jock and I could see that autumn publication was now more than a possibility. He promised to use every possible means of publicity – a promise he faithfully and generously kept so long as Geoffrey Bles was publishing the translation. When the publishing passed to Collins it was reported to me that the sales of *The New Testament in Modern English* dropped dramatically. As I and others were constantly receiving letters from both schools and individuals asking for copies or wondering why it was allowed to go out of print, I could only conclude that this was due to the lack of publicity. Sales continued to be high in America for many years.

Publicity for *The Young Church in Action*

Later in the afternoon I went to have a publicity photograph taken by the distinguished London photographer, Mark Gerson. Strangely enough the sitter before me had been one whom I greatly admired, Stella Gibbons. She had apparently wondered aloud to Mr. Gerson why she had never again attained the fabulous success of *Cold Comfort Farm*. This unique magical *jeu d'esprit* cannot fail to remain as a classic for many years to come. I have myself read it twenty times or so and I marvel at its sure-footed audacity and unfaltering wit. Both my daughter and her husband (some forty years my junior) have also, to my intense delight, read it with every sign of joy.

I chiefly remember my own sitting with Mr. Gerson because one set of photographs was taken of me with a pipe and another set without. Those who know the American religious market will well know why. Incidentally I regard with some awe the well known photograph of C. S. Lewis, in which he has apparently just ignited a small bomb and is surrounded by the ensuing clouds of smoke. I am pretty sure I have seen this photograph in various parts of the U.S.A. as well as over here.

In early autumn I heard that my *Young Church in Action* was being printed, that there was a huge advance order, and that the staff at Geoffrey Bles were hard at work, parcelling and addressing. On an impulse of pure gratitude I went up to London to thank them. I was amazed at the sight. Every member of the staff of that high and narrow house at 52 Doughty Street, was hard at work. From the lowliest office boy to the highest and most expert secretary every one was doing manual labour. In every space on all floors, and even on the staircases, were pile upon pile of *my book*, while every so often vans called to deliver hundreds of books to the London bookshops and stores. I was enormously grateful, and I did my honest best to thank every single one of Bles' army.

Only a week or two later I came again to London for publication day, I can remember having lunch with my brother Kenneth at the National Book League (my only London club) and then bussing and walking to St. Paul's. There are quite a number of bookshops in that area and all of them had a large window display of the *Young Church in Action* and my other works, decorated with a life-sized enlargement of the Mark Gerson photograph. I cannot now remember quite where I had promised to autograph books, but it was at a small number of shops, and indeed not very many people actually came for my autograph. Nevertheless it was a day to be remembered.

The newborn Church

It is impossible to spend several months in close study of the Acts of the Apostles, without being profoundly stirred and, to be honest, disturbed. The reader is stirred because he is seeing Christianity, the real thing, in action for the first time in human history. The newborn Church, as vulnerable as any human child, having neither money and influence nor power in the ordinary sense, is setting forth joyfully and courageously to win the pagan world for God through Christ. The young Church, like all young creatures, is appealing in its simplicity and singleheartedness. Here we are seeing the Church in its first youth, valiant and unspoilt – a body of ordinary men and women joined in an unconquerable fellowship never before seen on earth.

Yet we cannot help feeling disturbed as well as moved, for this surely is the Church as it was meant to be. It is vigorous and flexible, for these are the days before it ever became fat and short of breath through prosperity, or muscle-bound by over-organisation. These men did not make acts of faith, they believed; they did not "say their prayers", they really prayed. They did not hold conferences on psychosomatic medicine; they simply healed the sick. But if they were uncomplicated and naive by modern standards we have ruefully to admit that they were open on the God-ward side in a way that is almost unknown today.

No one can read this book without being convinced that there is Someone here at work besides mere human beings. Perhaps because of their very simplicity, perhaps because of their readiness to believe, to obey, to give, to suffer, and if need be to die, the Spirit of God found what surely he must always be seeking – a fellowship of men and women so united in love and faith that he can work in them and through them with the minimum of let or hindrance. Consequently it is a matter of sober historical fact that never before has any small body of ordinary people so moved the world that their enemies could say, with tears of rage in their eyes, that these men "have turned the world upside down".

In the pages of this unpretentious second book, written by the author of the third gospel, the fresh air of Heaven is plainly blowing, and to turn from the vitality of these pages to almost any current Christian writing, be it a theological book or a Church periodical, is to bring tears to Christian eyes. Of course the moment one suggests that our tragically divided and tradition-choked Church might learn from this early unsophistication, one is accused of over-simplification of the issues involved in our modern world. But it should be remembered that the ancient world was not without its complex problems also. It is of course possible that the translator has had his head turned by too close a study of these artless and energetic pages, but nevertheless he feels after such study that the Holy Spirit has a way of short-circuiting human problems. Indeed, in exactly the same way as Jesus Christ in the flesh cut right through the matted layers of tradition and exposed the real issue; just as he again and again brought down a theoretical problem to a personal issue, so we find here the Spirit of Jesus dealing not so much with problems as with people.

Broadcasting

Between those two visits to London, in connection with the publication of *The Young Church in Action*, one in the spring, appropriately enough a visit of hope and expectation, and the other in the autumn, with a similar felicity, to see the fruits of my labours, a vast amount of work of various kinds, appeared on my desk that year.

I made one of my visits to the B.B.C. in Bristol, and arranged with Martin Wilson to make some short contributions. B.B.C. Bristol in those days was comparatively small. Everybody was most kind and there was a strong family feeling which I suppose is inevitably lost when a unit becomes much larger. Today, because of the vast improvements in tape-recording, a great many talks and interviews are pre-recorded – sometimes on very small (but highly expensive) battery recorders. The fidelity to the original is astounding. Thus today if I am asked to broadcast, a B.B.C. sound engineer calls on me with his little lightweight apparatus, and there is no fuss and the minimum consumption of time. But in 1954 I had to drive to Bristol (some ninety miles), make my recording and then drive back to Swanage. The return journey was always well after darkness had fallen. These talks were subsequently published as a small book by the Lutterworth Press under the title, *When God was Man*.

In the spring of 1955 I visited the television studios of the B.B.C. in Lime Grove. I am not quite sure why I was invited, but a scheme was being planned to write and produce a "life of Jesus" for children's T.V. I expect I was there in a sort of advisory capacity, for I remember being asked a lot of questions and taking part in much lively and friendly discussion. The series was eventually written by Joy Harington and produced with great care and skill. I watched it faithfully but, although it was difficult to fault, to me it lacked any challenge or cutting edge.

Somewhere about this time I prepared several tapes for the Australian Broadcasting Commission at the invitation of the Reverend Kenneth Henderson, whom I had previously met at St. Julian's. These I tape-recorded on my own "professional" tape-recorder with my wife acting (as so often in later years) as time-keeper and engineer. These were apparently well received and I had an encouraging bunch of letters from that vast continent. Indeed one or two contacts have been maintained to this day. One in particular is Mrs. Amy Groves, who has written to me scores of letters over the years. She must be getting well on in years by now, but despite her curious way of writing in "telegraphese" every letter is full of indomitable faith and childlike joy in every good gift of God. She and her husband Sam have known trouble in plenty, but there is never a word or even a hint of impatience or doubt. Strangely, she has a peculiar gift of knowing when I am going through a particularly dark and painful time and she writes accordingly. I look forward to meeting her either in this world or the next.

Oxford

In June I went to Oxford at the invitation of an old Cambridge friend, the Reverend Oscar Keith de la Tour de Berry. He was vicar of St. Aldate's, an evangelical stronghold, and I preached what I thought was a strong and provocative message. I knew very well that the bulk of my hearers would be ardent members of the Oxford Christian Union. But I also realised that there would be a number who would be there to see and hear a man who was beginning to be a world-famous translator! I took a lot of time and trouble in preparing this address, but to this day I have never heard of the slightest result.

An American interlude

During the summer of 1955 we were happy to welcome to Swanage some American visitors. One of the ministers of the Presbyterian church in Hollywood, the Reverend (now Dr.) Walt James with his charming wife Marguerite came to stay with us for a few days. They had housed and fed us in their own home while we were in Hollywood at some sacrifice to themselves, and we were delighted to do something to repay them. They were enchanted with this beautiful country, and almost overwhelmed by the loveliness of one of the few abbeys which was spared by Henry VIII – that at Sherborne. I don't think it was mere politeness which made them say that they were so happy with British ways. The nearness of the "ocean" (as they always called the English Channel), the extreme clarity of the atmosphere and the soft greens of the countryside filled them with delight. They found, according to their light-meter (which all Americans carry) that the light value here was the same as in an outdoor set in Hollywood, which is not to be wondered at since there is no industry nearer than thirty miles. Little things like the greenness of our lawn (which was actually at that time pretty rough) amazed and charmed them, and so did the traffic-free secondary roads on which we drove to show them something of this (still) unspoilt county.

One little incident amused me. For most of our married life Vera and I had lived as rigid teetotallers, not through conviction but simply because we could not afford even a bottle of sherry. However by now we could easily afford a social drink now and again and although we drank, and drink, very little we do enjoy, say, a glass of sherry before a meal. It so happened that in our travels with Walt and Marguerite we stopped for lunch at the Digby hotel in Sherborne. We suggested various harmless drinks, all politely refused, until we mentioned cider. This, apparently, was O.K. with them. I did not think this was the moment to point out that a glass of Dorset cider contains at least as much alcohol as a small glass of sherry, nor to draw attention to the fact that there is a very potent cider obtainable hereabouts (known as vintage cider) which is so powerful that the ordinary publican will allow you no more than a quarter of a pint. Anyway the cider was duly ordered and enjoyed by Walt and Marguerite and we had a most happy luncheon party.

Harvest in Sheffield

In September I accepted an invitation from the Reverend Murray Penfold to preach harvest sermons for him in his church in Sheffield. I had paid many visits to Yorkshire but I had never seen a place so heavily industrialised. I must confess my heart sank as my host drove me from the station to his old-fashioned and fiendishly inconvenient vicarage. If there was a blade of grass, a flower or a tree to be seen my eye failed to catch any of them. The atmosphere was, to my nose, eyes and throat terribly polluted, although the Penfold family had long grown used to it. Indeed Mrs. Penfold assured me that the sulphurous, and other, fumes in the atmosphere actually helped her chronic asthma! She felt better in Sheffield than anywhere else. There was one tree in the vicarage garden, and someone told me that when it blossomed in spring many people of that parish would take a special walk just to see it in bloom. I can well believe it.

But if the atmosphere was polluted and the general outlook grim, there was no lack of north country warmth in the life of that church. I was given a great welcome and although the massed flowers and piled fruits and vegetables seemed a little incongruous in such grey and dismal surroundings, there was plenty of genuine joy in the hearty singing of the traditional harvest hymns. Of course, these good Yorkshire folk knew that despite their immediate surroundings the genuine countryside was in truth near at hand. I did not know this on the Sunday, but on Monday I soon saw that a very few minutes in a car led me to the splendid hills and crags, moors and fells of the stirring Yorkshire scene.

A tribute to my brother

On Bible Sunday I preached for my brother, the Reverend (later Canon) K. C. Phillips. I have admired my brother for many years. Long ago we used to say in jest that "I was the one who talked and wrote about things; he was the one who did them." He served as a missionary in the Szechwan province of Old China before the war, became an R.A.F. padre largely in the Burma campaign, was mentioned in despatches and on being demobilised was given a drab and difficult job in Coventry. From there he went to Sydenham in south-east London, occupying the most tumbledown and ramshackle vicarage I have ever seen, although he and his wife never complained. And it was in Sydenham in a vast church that I preached in 1955. Three years later I was to preach again for him in his charming old church at Woking, at last living in a modern comfortable vicarage, and being paid something like a living wage.

Alas, within a few years he was stricken with multiple sclerosis and thus forced to resign the living. Nevertheless, despite all the handicaps which a wheelchair imposes, he continued as Woking's rural dean for several more years travelling around the parishes in his adapted car, and preaching whenever he was invited – and that was pretty often. He still cheerfully continued his limited ministry and lived in a bungalow at Pyrford not far from Woking itself. I was proud to have such a brother. He died in 1977 and many tributes were justly paid to him at his memorial service.

Worldwide correspondence

In 1955 there was a large daily correspondence, increasingly from the U.S.A. Sometimes the letters were simple enough and could be answered shortly and easily. But others raised deep questions of the nature of God, of scripture and of all the great issues of the Christian faith. Rightly or wrongly I felt bound to answer all these as well as I could, tiresome as some of them were.

Many of the letters came from those in the prime of life, some of whom had high intellectual qualifications and some who were quite ordinary people. They came from all parts of the world, letters from six continents. I have made a selection from some of these and have taken them from different countries and from different subjects:

A correspondent from America wrote sending me an article which was highly critical of my translations. Reading the article carefully I replied:

Thank you for sending me the criticisms of my translational work by Professor George P. Black. He seems to me to be either very prejudiced or very ignorant of what translation really means! You cannot take Greek words and render them by English equivalents. I have a whole-hearted admiration for the Authorised Version, but even these translators of 347 years ago did not fall into that kind of error! For example, they did not hesitate to translate "the wineskins" of Matthew 9:17 as "bottles", nor did they hesitate to change the Eastern habit of reclining at meals into "sitting at meat". What is more they translated the Greek word *ekballo* variously; it is "pluck out" (Mt. 7:5); "cast out" (Mt. 8:12); "put out" (Mt. 9:25); "put forth" (Mt. 12:35); etc. etc. But, bless their hearts, these translators had more wit and good sense than Dr. Black and were not tied by his theories of what constitutes good translation. I wonder what he makes of the oddities of N.T. Greek in the Book of Revelation! I also wonder whether he realises that the beauty and majesty of the A.V. lovely and admirable as they are, are in no sense a real translation of the somewhat pedestrian *koine* of most of the N.T.

From Queensland, Australia came a request for help in learning N.T. Greek.

I have read your translation of the gospels. I much prefer it to any translation I have ever read.

For a long time I have wanted to read the gospels in the original Greek. Your aims in translation have inspired me to write to you to ask you to recommend some books which I could use to teach myself to read the gospels in the original.

I recommended three books.

From Brazil came a complaint about my translation of ceremonial washing:

Reading your book *The Gospels in Modern English* I see that in Luke 11:38 you have "When the Pharisee noticed this, he was surprised that he did not *wash* before the meal" so following the A.V. and many modern translators, and giving the deplorable suggestion that Jesus sat down to table *dirty*. This is entirely avoided in Young's Literal Translation: "the Pharisee having seen, did wonder that he did not first *baptize* himself before the dinner." Also an exact translation "baptize himself" gives a valuable clue to the sort of baptizing spoken of in the ceremonial sprinkling which the Pharisee would expect to see each guest do as he passed the stone (?) water-pots for the purifying of the Jews.

I replied as simply as I could:

Thank you for your letter of the 14th May. I think it would be extremely misleading for a translator to use the expression "baptize himself" instead of "wash" in Luke 11:38. I know very well that the Pharisees used a certain kind of ceremonial washing, which apparently Jesus omitted before the meal. But surely the place to draw attention to this is in a commentary and not in a straightforward translation. I have before me the latest inter-linear New Testament published a week or so ago by Messrs. Samuel Bagster and Sons of London. Dr. Alfred Marshall supplies a literal translation between the lines of Greek text. He uses "wash" and not the word "baptize" in this passage simply because,

I imagine, to use the word "baptize" would be misleading. Unless a translator is going to overload his work with footnotes, he is bound to simplify for the modern reader. Any serious student of the New Testament would naturally consult a commentary.

I sometimes had more than one letter and kept up a correspondence with a Ghanaian who was worried about the "The Akan Doctrine of God". Such a letter required a great deal of work as it had to be replied to in some detail:

The revolutionary thought in St. Paul is that God is no longer the External Power whose Perfection can never be remotely approached by sinful human beings, but that He is the God who personally made the reconciliation between man and God. (Vide 2 Cor. 5:18–21; and Col. 2:13–15.) This action of God, demonstrated by the Cross and Resurrection of Jesus, is the outcrop in time of God's eternal attitude towards mankind. For Saul the Pharisee God was always to be feared because the condemnation of God's Law hung over his head. But to Paul the Christian God has been revealed as Love, personally breaking the sin-guilt-fear-death complex of sinful mankind. This is revolutionary teaching and is unique to Christianity. Once a man has realised that the true God is not the fearful Avenger of his own conscience, but Love-in-action, to go on sinning is unspeakable, it is what he calls "a ghastly thought". To believe with heart and mind that the Character of God is what I have just described makes it impossible to go on living a self-pleasing life. The soul which had been awakened by the Love of God responds in love and obedience to the revealed pattern of God's Will. Naturally this is not a matter of believing a certain theory, which may mean no more than giving intellectual assent, but committal of the whole life to a new way of living, which is probably what Paul meant when he said "to me to live is Christ".

I was in trouble from Ethiopia where fasting is so important because I had translated prayer and fasting simply as prayer:

On behalf of my schoolmates, and teacher, I would like to tell you that we enjoy much your new translation of the Gospels, which we are studying in our class.

So as we went on reading and discussing the Gospel of Mark, we came to a point where there was something important dropped in a verse. And that is the Gospel of Mark chapter 9 verse 28–29. In the English Gospel it is written "And when He was come into the house, his disciples asked him privately, why could not we cast him out? And he said unto them, "This kind can come forth by nothing but by *prayer* and *fasting.*" But in your book it is written, 'Nothing can drive out this kind of thing except *prayer'*, replied Jesus." But not the word *fasting*.

May we trouble you with a question? Why was it left out? Is it not in the original Greek, or what is the reason?

From Bruce Rock, Australia, came a complaint from a member of the Churches of Christ that the local Anglican clergyman had been less than charitable. I sympathised with him and said so.

I was much encouraged by many of these letters. As the years passed this correspondence ministry grew and was greatly increased after the publication of *Ring of Truth* in 1967.

Requests to speak
1955 also saw the beginning of that huge and alarming avalanche of requests to speak which continued for several years and has not altogether ceased today. At first (how naive can you be?) I thought every request was of the nature of a divine command. But quite soon this was plainly absurd. When invitations to speak, lecture or preach began to reach the 300-a-year mark even I could see that this could hardly be part of the divine plan. I had made this drastic change in my lifestyle after much prayer and consultation with wise friends, and it would be nonsensical to allow this specialised ministry to be smothered and stultified by continual travelling and speaking. I was forced to be discriminating. My priorities were, in random order: adolescents, whether in school groups or not, young people, meetings of clergy and minis-

ters and opportunities of broadcasting (this because of the sheer number one can speak to simultaneously), and meetings concerned with the spread of the Bible in translation.

12

A Varied Ministry
1956–1958

I was working to the limit of my strength in writing, speaking and answering a very considerable correspondence. Some of the latter raised personal and spiritual problems and I did my best to give good counsel. I must confess that sometimes I felt like replying, "Why don't you consult your own vicar, minister or pastor?" But I had constantly to remind myself that both North America and Australia are lands of huge distances; it was perfectly possible that the nearest professional counsellor was a hundred miles away or more. Whether I was right or wrong I took it as my duty to dispense advice, comfort and reassurance whenever I was asked for such things.

Advice to would-be authors

Both in 1956 and in the ensuing years I received quite a number of manuscripts from would-be authors, asking for my opinion and advice. I felt it only fair to read all these and make such suggestions as I could. Some were, frankly, quite hopeless. Not only did they fail to say anything new or relevant but they said, in fact, nothing at all. It took all my reserves of tact to tell this to the authors kindly and truthfully. Some, however, had some merit, but the authors, being the merest amateurs, had naturally no idea how to shape their work to make it acceptable and, no less important in the world of publishing, marketable. I like to think that I was of some service to these men and women writers. At any rate I was always, I think, just and kind.

Then came, and this continues to this day, the requests for

permission to quote. The general rule is that if you are quoting a few lines only and the source is acknowledged no permission is required from either me or from the copyright holder, who is usually the publisher. But when a man proposes (as did happen once) to construct a life of Jesus by cutting out chunks of my translation of the four gospels and then re-assembling them (a real scissors and paste job) then he must expect to pay a proper copyright fee. He must also, in this instance anyway, expect to meet severe discouragement. But no translator, I believe, would dream of expecting a fee when his work is used within the framework of a normal church service.

The Church under the Cross

In addition to all my normal writing and correspondence two important events that year, 1956, stand out in my mind: first, writing another book for the Church Missionary Society, and the other the conducting of the mission to Dorking.

I had for many years been keen on missionary work, and I welcomed the opportunity of doing something concrete for an often despised, but to my mind courageous and valuable part of the Church's work in the world. So I went up to C.M.S. headquarters in London (then in Salisbury Square) and discussed the matter. The quarrying of suitable material from letters and reports from various parts of the world would be done for me. Then it was my job to use this material and turn it into a popular, readable book with the title, *The Church under the Cross*. It took me three months and it was hard concentrated work, but I understand that the book was, in the right sense, popular and sold well.

In those days the C.M.S. had their own publishing house, the Highway Press. I gave the typescript of this book and of the earlier one, *Making Men Whole* to the Highway Press. To this day I do not know how much money the C.M.S. gained from these two books, but it must have been a considerable sum, and I am glad. Incidentally I learnt indirectly from C. S. Lewis that if you want to give away the proceeds of a book you do not sign a contract and then give the object of your good intentions the royalties. That way you pay income tax (and possibly surtax) on the gross royalties. But if you sign no contract but give the typescript to the organisation of your concern then they draw the royalties, and being a registered charity, pay no tax at all. C. S. Lewis in his generosity gave away the royalties of, I think, *The Problem of Pain* to some deserving cause, only to find that he had to pay tax just the same.

The Dorking mission

In the early Summer came the Dorking Mission, a seven-day week of evening addresses by me followed by informal questions-and-answers from any who stayed behind. This was my other major undertaking of that year. Every night the church in Dorking was well filled and I could not have wished for a more attentive audience. On the closing Sunday we decided not to have any emotional "stand up for Jesus" business, but instead to ask those who wanted to follow, and know more of the way of Jesus Christ, to fill in a card. These cards were collected and placed on the altar with suitable prayer. Rather to my surprise somewhere around 170 men and women expressed their serious interest in and/or commitment to the Christian faith. This is quite a large number for a small town like Dorking, and each of these possibles was followed up faithfully by the clergy, and sometimes the laity, of that rural town. From what I heard afterwards a good deal of seed had fallen on good ground.

Published lectures

New Testament Christianity was published early in 1956 by Hodder & Stoughton, and drew from C. S. Lewis the comment, "It has great freshness and energy and I particularly liked the way it deals with faith – a very helpful approach." It was not particularly arduous work for the material was the fruit of the lectures I had given at the Forest Home conference, near Hollywood, and which were repeated at the similar gathering at Lake Tahoe. It was a matter of turning the spoken word into the written word, and, although there is quite a difference between the two methods of communication, it did not prove difficult for me to transform them into chapters of a book. *New Testament Christianity* was an instant success on both sides of the Atlantic (Macmillans being my New York publisher). Before long it became a paperback and sold more than 100,000 copies. Much more importantly, it revived interest in the Christian faith, especially to those for whom it had become a dead and formal thing. By the grace of God hundreds were stimulated and illuminated. In the nature of things my own mail was but a small sample, but this was large enough.

Return visits

Among other engagements of that crowded year, 1956, I preached at the harvest services in the church of the Good Shepherd, Lee, where I had been vicar. The church was not yet re-built, but as usual the spirit of the people was warm, welcoming and enthusiastic. They had not very long to wait before a fine new church was finished. I also had the very great pleasure of speaking in the chapel of my old Cambridge college, Emmanuel. After the service I dined, for the first time in my life, at the High Table and afterwards adjourned to the Combination Room. Here I was delighted to find my Classics tutor, L. H. G. Greenwood, now retired but visiting England from his native New Zealand. He had taught me a lot about Greek and its proper translation; I fear my few words of gratitude were hardly adequate for the great debt I owed to him.

Revelation

The bulk of my work on the translation of the Book of Revelation was done in this very full year. In some ways it was the most difficult piece of translation I had so far tackled. It proved to be at close quarters a very impressive piece of what we might call high, celestial poetry. Purely literal translation would destroy all the sense of mystery and awe which pervade the book. Yet I felt it my duty to remove obscurity and correct the few obvious errors which appear in the 1611 translation.

I wrote in the preface: "Once one had absorbed the initial shock of the peculiar Greek, the effect of the language of this book is most powerful. The crowns, the thrones, the jewels, the colours, the trumpets, the violence of action and the impact of incredible numbers and awe-inspiring size – all these images stir that threshold of the brain where monsters lurk and the supernatural glories blaze."

However, certain themes emerge distinctly for the modern reader's profit:

(a) The absolute sovereignty of God, and his ultimate purpose to destroy all forms of evil.

(b) The inevitable judgments of God upon evil, upon the worship of false gods, which include riches, power and success.

(c) The necessity for patient endurance, the ultimate security being the knowledge that God is in control of history.

(d) The existence of reality, represented here under such symbols as the New Jerusalem, set apart and secure from the battles and tribulations of earthly life, promises complete spiritual security to those who are faithful to God and his Christ.

(e) The glimpses of worship and adoration, constantly offered to God and the Lamb, are a kind of pattern of man's ultimate acknowledgment of the character of God when he sees him as he is.

But for any proper appreciation of the themes of this mysterious book it is imperative that the reader should make use of one or more commentaries.

The translation was well reviewed, and I particularly valued some appreciative words written by the late G. K. A. Bell, then Bishop of Chichester. He wrote: "It is admirable. There is no lessening of the mystery, but the version is written in so clear and vivid a style that the reader cannot fail to be entranced and enthralled."

Dr. Bell had made me a prebendary of Chichester, with the idea, he said with a twinkle in the eye, that "I might do for the Prayer Book what I had done for the New Testament!" I did indeed begin some rough drafts, but before anything serious could be established he retired and then not very long afterwards died. The question was not raised by his successor, and since the journey from here to Chichester was excessively tedious (and in the summer almost impossible) I felt bound to resign the prebend in 1960.

U.S. air force mission

One of the most memorable experiences of 1957 was the mission to the U.S.A.F. at Bentwaters in wildest Suffolk. I decided to go by train and be met at some station, which I have now forgotten, by U.S. transport. On that journey I studied my permit. (I must say in passing that I rather resented the fact that I, an Englishman, should have to have permission from the Pentagon to enter a part of my own country, temporarily occupied by the U.S.A.) My official permit stated that I was entitled to transport, by air if necessary etc. I immediately decided that I would avail myself of this facility for the homeward journey, which indeed took the better part of a day.

I was very well treated by the Americans whether airmen or civilians. The mission itself consisted of a week of evening meetings, followed by discussion or counselling. All these gatherings were well attended and I was listened to with close attention. As at the Dorking mission I set out what I believed to be an intelligent outline of the Christian faith. A lot of interest was aroused and I was asked a number of intelligent questions. As far as I can judge the mission opened the eyes of quite a number, and confirmed the faith of others.

The commanding officer of the station was Colonel John Robie, a fine-looking character with lots of personality. I believe he attended the meetings at first to set a good example but towards the end of the week it was plain that he was deeply interested. On the last evening of the mission he came round to see me and handed me a signed photograph with the words "I will" written above his signature. Before shaking hands with me he said a few brief words (he was not at any time verbose) indicating that he had made an important decision. How important I did not know at the time.

Somewhat tired but on the whole feeling that the effort was well worth it, I packed up for my return journey. "Could I be flown home – to Hurn airport, only a few miles from my home?" "Why sure, sure, no trouble at all." And then a few

minutes later, "Padre, do you mind going via Manchester –
we've got a few of the boys for leave to drop off there?" Of
course I didn't mind. Even via Manchester the journey would
be infinitely quicker than the wearisome cross-country journey by train. So we embarked with half a dozen or so lower
ranking airmen, with naturally a pilot and co-pilot. The first
leg of this journey was very formal. Not only were we strap-
ped in but we each sat on a parachute and were told how to
use it. The journey of about 170 miles took not much over an
hour.

Then, having dismissed the troops, we settled down in
comfort. Such frivolities as safety straps and parachutes were
discarded, I was allowed to sit between pilot and co-pilot and
to wear a spare set of headphones. I have never been afraid of
flying but this little journey dispelled any lingering doubts. I
had not realised before that the ground would be talking to us
every few minutes. We were flying in ten-tenths cloud and
couldn't see a thing. But every few minutes one of a series of
kindly efficient voices would tell us where we were, what was
our actual height, what was our true speed and compass
bearing. Not long after leaving Manchester (in fact an hour
before we landed) the pilot called Hurn airport and asked for
permission to land, which was readily given. I had previously
telephoned my wife and asked her to meet me at the airport,
which she agreed to do. She arrived at what appeared to be an
utterly deserted airfield (as Hurn was in those days out of
season). Eventually she found someone and, "No, he knew
nothing about an American plane due to arrive that day, but
their radio was permanently on etc." However soon afterwards he received a call and told my wife our expected time of
arrival.

Meantime, back in the rather ageing Dakota (I noted that it
had been made in Oklahoma in 1943) we could see nothing
outside the plane itself. However before long the pilot was
speaking to the flight controller at Hurn. The reply was, "You
are 1,000 feet up, air speed 135 knots, start coming down . . .
coming down . . . and you should see the landing lights *now!*"
And we did, and made a perfect landing. This was travelling
without any trouble at all; especially when a welcoming wife

was waiting beside the runway. I hope I expressed adequately my gratitude to the U.S. pilots.

But to return to Colonel Robie. He wrote to me some weeks after the mission to tell me that a dramatic improvement had set in all over the station. Petty crime was now very small and serious misdemeanours had vanished entirely. In fact he, the commanding officer was likely to be in trouble because he was taking such greatly diminished disciplinary action!

Later he and his wife came down to see me. We talked quite a lot and he told me he was considering resigning his commission and taking on some specifically Christian work. This he did before long and when last I heard he was doing life- and soul-saving work in one of the unsavoury areas of New York. Alas, we have lost touch over the years with one of the best men it has been my privilege to know.

A man called Jesus

In 1958 I was asked by the B.B.C. if I would prepare twenty-six scripts for sound radio, each limited to eight minutes, on the life of Jesus. I went to London to consult with Robert Walton who was in charge of religious programmes broadcast to schools. Between us we mapped out roughly what each interlude should contain. I worked pretty fast in those days and in a matter of a few weeks the dramatic episodes were complete.

I think it was not until the next year that the little plays were rehearsed and later broadcast. Vera and I went up to Broadcasting House to see some of the rehearsal, and were astounded at the immense pains taken by the producer to secure near perfection. The B.B.C. also employed first-rate actors and actresses and between them and careful production the result far exceeded my most optimistic hopes. I chiefly remember such people as Fay Compton and Deryck Guyler but even the smallest bit-part was expertly rehearsed and played. We found to our great surprise that it took the whole of a working day to satisfy the producer over only two eight-minute interludes.

The scripts attracted great attention and led to requests by amateur actors for permission to produce the plays. I was only too glad to give this permission but I had no copies available. It was not until 1959 that the plays were published in hardback (and later in paperback) book form under the title of *A Man Called Jesus*. These plays sold very well and were most flatteringly reviewed. Correspondents from various parts of the country assured me that they were most effective for amateur production. It was therefore decided to produce an acting edition, which would give practical hints on costume, lighting and sound effects. This task was undertaken by an experienced actress, a friend of Jock Gibb, whose name was Pamela Sinclair. I was not an official proofreader but I read the practical hints with interest and appreciation. I did not check the cast or the dialogue as I assumed no change would be made. Some years later I was horrified to discover that Pamela Sinclair had added the characters of Luke and Mark to the scene of the Last Supper. Neither, of course, could possibly have been present and neither were apostles! I blame myself for not noticing this error before, but it is difficult to the point of impossibility to correct an error in a long run of paperbacks.

Apart from this sad error, the most lasting disappointment was that the B.B.C. had not preserved the tapes. If I had known that erasure was to take place within a very short time I could easily have taped the beautifully acted scenes myself. Requests for such recordings have been quite frequent, some for re-broadcasting in the U.S.A., for example, and some for producers of amateur groups in various places. I still have one or two scenes, rather imperfectly recorded by a friend. The scene of the weeping Mary at the empty tomb can still move me to tears. The part of Mary was played by the incomparable Fay Compton.

The New Testament in Modern English

With the whole of the New Testament now translated in separate volumes my mind, and Jock Gibb's, began to think of presenting them all in one volume. It was a good opportunity to make some (not very drastic) revisions. At intervals during a very busy year I would take a complete day to read, listen to and examine every word and phrase which I had used. The book was ready to be published in 1958. A month or two after the publication here Macmillans of New York mounted a huge publicity campaign in the U.S.A. They invited me to spend a three-week holiday in the States in the fall, and this advertising campaign was in full swing when we visited New England towards the end of September. They were able to say that a million copies of my books had been sold. This included 809,000 of the translations and 217,000 of the other books. They had spent $30,000 on the advertising campaign in newspapers, magazines and journals with a combined circulation of 26,000,000. This did not of course include the British sales which, by the end of 1958 were half a million for the translation alone. By 1972 Fontana sales were over 1,750,000.

Scotland

In the autumn I travelled to Scotland to preach for a Presbyterian minister, James Currie. He and a colleague were in charge of a new estate in Glasgow called Pollok. James and his delightful wife, Peggy, have become over the years two of our most valued friends. It was while staying with the Curries that I was interviewed by a B.B.C. reporter, Glen Gibson. He was a skilled interviewer and I was ready enough to answer intelligent questions about translation from New Testament Greek into today's English. The thought of being *paid* for what was really a friendly chat never entered my head, but in due course I received a cheque for fifteen guineas. The dialogue which was originally broadcast on the Scottish Home Service, was repeated at least twice in the following months (I presume for use in other regions) and each time I received a repeat fee of half the original amount. Never have I earnt money so easily.

From the outskirts of Glasgow Vera and I travelled to Edinburgh, where I had been booked for some months to preach in St. Giles Cathedral. Ignorant as I was, I did not know that there were *two* cathedrals in Edinburgh, one Episcopalian and one Presbyterian. I suppose I had imagined that all cathedrals were Anglican. I was a little shaken to find that St. Giles was a stronghold of Presbyterians. When sermontime came I held forth blithely enough, on "Some Difficulties of Translation". I did not realise until afterwards that many of the reverend, grave and elderly men who sat under the pulpit were some of Scotland's leading New Testament scholars. However I was courteously received and warmly thanked.

Within the Royal Navy

In January of 1958 I accepted an invitation to be one of a panel of speakers in a Christian Forum. It was to be held at the Royal Naval aircraft station at Culdrose, towards Land's End in Cornwall. It was a fair distance away, and Vera and I decided to take two days for the journey. As events turned out it was just as well that we did. For as we approached Axminster and were just about to cross the Dorset-Devon border, the road suddenly became covered with a sheet of ice. I have had a good deal of experience in driving and am accustomed to most road hazards. I can correct any ordinary skid as swiftly as the next man, but I defy anyone to exert anything but minimal control when the road is a continuous sheet of ice. I knew all the tricks but none of them is of any use when none of your wheels has any true contact with the road. It makes you feel singularly helpless to find that the brake-pedal has no effect whatever and turning the steering-wheel, however gingerly, makes no difference to your direction of movement at all. Fortunately there was little traffic about but I knew there was a longish hill down into Axminster. Devon twenty years ago was not organised for ice, for it freezes very rarely; there were no handy piles of road-grit to be seen. By every device I could muster I managed to reduce our speed, but even so, as we slid down that hill we were as often broadside on as facing forwards, and we missed a huge truck crawling up the hill by mere inches. Once in Axminster we made a frantic search for chains and happily managed to get some a mile or so out of the town. We pressed on, with occasional frightening total loss of ability to steer, and when we got to Exeter we decided to stay the night at an hotel there, and complete the journey by train.

The hotel was packed, mostly with travellers like ourselves who had been caught by the sudden and unexpected freeze. There were also some of the Christian Forum itself, including our chairman Alan Gibson (still my favourite sports commentator). I remember discussing with Alan during the long train journey next day the merits and demerits of well known hymns.

We finally arrived at some remote Cornish station, where a Royal Navy van was waiting to take us on to Culdrose. It was very cold and there was ice both inside and outside the windows. The driver had rubbed himself a small oblong visibility patch in the frozen windscreen, and we were driven at a smart clip between hedges rigid with frost while snow was falling heavily. However we arrived safely at the naval base and were warmly welcomed, and later, as all Britons expect from the senior service, royally entertained. Father Agnellus Andrew and a Congregational minister, Noel Calvin, and one other whom I cannot recall, were all present.

Later on, in March, I was asked to take part in another Christian Forum. This one was to be held in a small stately home, at Urchfont Manor, near Devizes. Again Alan Gibson was in the chair and Edwin Robertson was a staunch ally for the Christian point of view. One member of the opposition was that able and witty personality, Marghanita Laski. I have a great respect for her, even though I cannot for a moment accept her atheism. My chief memory of this occasion was the extreme discomfort of the heat of the lights. Miss Laski was even then experienced, and wore the lightest of clothing; Edwin and I were in sober clerical grey. All windows had to be kept shut because of the noise of the B.B.C.'s generators which supplied electricity for the broadcast, and a fire was kept burning in the old-fashioned fireplace for the sake, I presume, of atmosphere. I have never been so hot in my life, not even in California.

An American holiday

In September we embarked on the *Queen Mary* for the holiday generously promised to us by Macmillans of New York. The journey was comfortable although we ran through a hurricane early one morning and the official report, chalked on the noticeboard, said, "Seas precipitous; hove to from 2 a.m. till 4 a.m." The seas were still enormous and I thought it worth while photographing some of them. As I made to go on deck a most polite steward stopped me, "Excuse me sir," he said, "but mind how you go, the wind is still over ninety knots." I managed to get a few good snaps of the "precipitous" seas, with, I remember, the view-piece of the camera being driven fiercely into my eyesocket by the gale.

We docked in New York early in the morning on September 30th, four hours late and we found it absolutely maddening to have to wait at least another four hours before we disembarked. Naturally enough U.S. citizens went ahead of us but there seemed to be an unending stream of them, and of course they were laden down heavily with their purchases in Europe and the time they spent in the customs seemed unending.

Our New York editor, and by now firm friend, Guy Brown, was awaiting us with a superb car laid on by Macmillans. We were able to exchange greetings with Con Lanford (who had been chaplain in Bentwaters, Suffolk) but as soon as we could we escaped to the Hotel Grosvenor, where Macmillans had booked us most comfortable rooms. We did a little desultory shopping and had a meal at a Chinese restaurant, which had a devastating, if delayed, effect on my digestion.

Macmillans
The next day was largely spent in visiting Macmillans who were then on Fifth Avenue. They had mounted an enormous advertising campaign and gave me a kit to show what they were doing. I remember being told that one full-page, full-colour advertisement in *Look* magazine had cost as much as the President's annual salary. Certainly they had poured a great deal of enthusiasm, as well as several thousand dollars, to make sure that my translation was well known in every state of the Union. It was good to meet, and thank in person, the people who had made such an energetic effort. I think I managed to get around all departments and suitably expressed my appreciation and gratitude. Compared with one small terraced house (which was all Geoffrey Bles could show) the premises of Macmillans were impressive and indeed palatial. I felt I was touching at least the fringe of big business!

182

Social visits

Later that day, after a meal in Fifth Avenue, we drove to Guy Brown's flat, part of a Victorian house some forty miles from New York itself, near the Croton Dam. It was plain but comfortable and quiet. That night we had a splendid meal with some local friends of G.B.'s, the Wilsons. But in the early hours of next morning I was struck with what the doctor called mild dysentery which lasted for nearly twenty-four hours. He considered it to be the delayed action of the meal at the Chinese restaurant. It certainly couldn't have been the result of the excellent dinner at the Wilsons'. All I can say is that if what I endured was "mild", Heaven preserve me from dysentery in a severe form.

While we were staying in New York Guy Brown had managed to get us tickets for *My Fair Lady*. This was a most enjoyable entertainment starring the delectable Julie Andrews and that most competent actor Rex Harrison. It was interesting to note that Americans sitting near us did not readily get the point of the play as no American speaks Cockney and few drop their aitches. But the show was so brilliantly produced, the costumes so eye-catching and the musical level so wholly delightful that the audience was enchanted.

Before we set off on our tour proper I had to endure twenty-four hours of nothing but Canada Dry – I drank twenty-seven bottles of the stuff – presumably to avoid de-hydration and to avoid any possible re-infection. Then we were invited to dinner with the chairman of the Macmillan company, George Brett, and his wife. Conversation was a bit sticky since I knew nothing about the business world or sailing yachts with every conceivable electric and electronic gadgets, and these appeared to be George's favourite interests. Mrs. Brett dropped the names of Harold and Dorothy fairly frequently into the conversation. It took me some time to realise that she was rather more than hinting at her friendship with our then Prime Minister and his wife.

Guy Brown

We had decided that we wanted to see not ancient (youthful by English standards) monuments or buildings but something of early America. We mostly travelled in New York State, Vermont, New Hampshire, Massachusetts, Pennsylvania and Maine.

Guy Brown was unsurpassable, to meet him was to know instantly that you had met an honest man. But Guy was far more than we mean by that everyday phrase. Behind his formidable charm, his mocking half-cynical comments on life and his constant chuckles – yes, Guy was one of the few men I've ever known who really chuckled – there lay a basic integrity of mind and heart which belongs only to those who see life steadily and see it whole. Touch him at any point and you would not only arouse his ready wit but you would also touch what John Milton called "the complete steel' of uncompromising honesty. It was only after you had known Guy for some time that you realised that beneath all his outflowing goodness was a deep religious faith. It was because he was sure of the love of God that he could be so immensely tolerant of his fellow human beings.

The tour

I remember stopping in a place in Manchester in Vermont and going into a bookshop called Johnny Appleseed's Bookstore. (Johnny Appleseed is an American folk-hero who wandered through the New England states eating apples and planting seeds for future generations.) The owners of the store were thrilled to meet the author of *The New Testament in Modern English* and I was thrilled to hear that the wife of the proprietor had met the book in England during a visit to London only a few weeks previously, and that certain passages in it had helped her enormously, being understood for the first time.

One particular contrast we vividly remember was that one night we were staying at the Middlebury Inn, Vermont, and since the central heating was on (because it was mid-October) we were excessively hot – so hot that the wooden floor itself was unbearable to the naked foot. We asked for a change of room and got it, but it was not much better. Yet the very next night we booked in at a cabin up in the mountains near Indian Head, where it was snowing hard and there was no central heating. However the cabin owner unfroze the cold-water pipes for us and gave us plenty of logs to use in the old-fashioned stove. And we needed them. The most primitive instincts of self-preservation emerged and Vera and I took it in turns to feed the fire and thus keep alive throughout a freezing night.

One thing which struck us particularly was the enormous sense of space. There were vast tracts of land without a house or building of any kind in sight and no one wanted to buy any portion of them. We visited Guy Brown's brother Karl who lived in an old-fashioned house in New Hampshire surrounded by a considerable acreage of beautiful woods. But the land was not really saleable, for the cost of clearing the woods and undergrowth and dynamiting the huge boulders which dotted the property in some profusion were quite enough to discourage any possible purchaser. All his estate was surrounded by thousands of acres of similar primitive woodland.

Between hotels and motels we were most kindly invited to stay at Guy Brown's brother's or sister's. During this stay we were taken to meet a Dr. and Mrs. Appleyard who had a splendid home on the shores of Lake Winnipesaukee. We were entertained by their daughters, Linda (fifteen and a half) and Barbara (twelve and a half) who played expertly on clarinet and flute/piccolo respectively. These two young girls were friendly and articulate and it was a joy to find two such natural and normal young people.

After an excellent dinner I found myself in conversation with two rather stern-faced Americans, I judge of the old-fashioned sort. I tried to explain to them the British system of rates (local taxes to them). It seemed impossible for them to believe that the rate collector over here is a civil servant, and is paid a fixed salary bearing no relation to the amount collected. It did not seem to me to be tactful to point out that if you appoint a local tax collector and pay him by results, the way is wide open for bribery and corruption.

We finally settled very happily into a motel on Cook's

Island, on the rocky coast of Maine, and used that as a base for further exploration. I had not felt so relaxed in years. To lie on my bed in a comfortable cabin with a pleasant drink at hand, watching Guy Brown teaching Vera to play Canasta (making up the rules as he went along, I strongly suspect) seemed for the moment all that I could need by way of earthly peace.

The return

By October 20th our time was up and we returned to Guy Brown's flat to pack for our return by air from Idlewild (as it was then) airport. There was a rumour that the British Comet was coming back into service, but we had to travel by Viscount and arrived at dusk just in time to see the first of the new and improved Comets taxiing for take-off. It was altogether a splendid holiday and I am still grateful to Macmillans for making it possible; but even more to my editor and friend Guy Brown who chauffeured us throughout the enormously varied and extremely enjoyable trip in his own car, and did everything for our comfort and peace of mind.

We were met by car at London airport by my sister and brother-in-law Dr. Thornton Weekley. They lived in Bournemouth at the time and were kind enough to bring us back to our home.

13

Communicating
1959–1961

The whole business of communication is that of conveying an idea accurately from one mind to the minds of many. This is much easier for some people than it is for others. It seems obvious and yet experience shows that it's not plain to everyone, that effective communication depends upon two absolute necessities. First, to understand as fully as possible the idea you are trying to get across, and second, to understand the state of mind, including the prejudices, of your listeners or readers.

Limpley Stoke

1959 saw the beginning of three proposed conferences to be held at the hotel of Limpley Stoke, a small village a few miles out from Bath. Martin Willson and I felt that there was a serious failure to communicate the essence of the Christian faith to ordinary people, and we decided to invite some two dozen men and women, all distinguished in their separate fields. We wanted to hear frank opinions and assessments of the situation. Martin and I felt that the majority of ordinary good-hearted people were quite indifferent to, as well as ignorant of, all ordinary theology. We felt that on the whole the British character can only appreciate faith when it is expressed in works of compassion for other people. We took as our starting point the only picture of the Last Judgment given in the gospels, i.e. the last part of chapter 25 in Matthew's gospel. This is the famous "inasmuch" passage, where men and women are commended or condemned for the way in which they treated those who were in want, hungry or thirsty, sick or in prison. Christ declared that inasmuch as we responded, or failed to respond to human need so we were, in fact, treating him.

I was earning good money by this time and so we were able to book the whole hotel for a couple of days in the off-season. Unhappily I don't seem to have kept a list of our guests, but I do remember Edwin Robertson (still then at the B.B.C.), "Bill" Purcell, R. H. Ward (poet, writer and dramatist), Miss (now Dame) Diana Reader Harris (Head of Sherborne School for Girls), C. A. Joyce (who had then retired from his magnificent work amongst delinquent boys), John Neville (the actor and outstanding Christian), Noel Calvin (Congregational Minister and most effective broadcaster), Miss Yanovsky (then working for the Children's Society), David Skinner (ex-Fleet Street journalist and at that time curate in Bristol), Basil Hembry (farmer and most thoughtful Christian), Dr. Charley (a scientist), Austen Williams (Vicar of St. Martin-in-the-fields), and Bertram Mycock (then Industrial Reporter for the B.B.C.).

We enjoyed some stimulating and, I think, fruitful discussions. We did not at any time think we were producing a revolution in Christian thinking, and I think at most we felt we might be creating ripples in the pond.

Ripples from Limpley Stoke

Some of the intentions suggested at Limpley Stoke have survived and nearly all of them were sooner or later put into practice.

It was suggested that representation should be made to the B.B.C. to see that in World Refugee Year, or the following year, the Reith Lecturer should be asked to put some emphasis on the fact that we are all, at least potentially, brothers, and that compassion as well as cash-giving should implement our sympathy with the emerging Third World.

A suggestion was made that both B.B.C. and I.T.V. should be strongly urged to step up their road safety campaign. The terrible slaughter on the roads was surely the concern of us all.

It was suggested that an idea which had already proved workable should be practised more widely. This was the direct linkage of a live youth club with the local "Darby and Joan" club. This was reported to have elicited compassion and enthusiasm from the young people in one church youth club and was greatly appreciated by the old.

Someone expressed his enthusiasm for the idea that representations of youth clubs or groups should be enabled actually to visit refugee camps and return to speak of the crying need.

It was felt that in some live church areas a pilot survey should be made so that the actual needs of the community be discovered and that people willing to help should be informed.

It was thought that women's magazine editors (whose combined circulation is really enormous) should be approached tactfully and asked to convey more of a message of service to others than of being cheered and cosseted themselves.

Something should be done to establish and expand the idea of an order of volunteers. Members would be expected to do a definite amount of compassionate work, give a little money to a central fund for special needs, and meet at intervals to pool resources.

Churches should be insistently reminded to turn outward rather than inward. Willing hearts and minds should be shown how to express their concern within a given community.

The B.B.C. should be approached to see whether an eight-part serial could be broadcast on sound radio. It should have the pace and appeal of "Dick Barton – Special Agent" but its dominant theme should be practical compassion.

R. H. Ward made several suggestions about a possible T.V. play showing the working out of compassion in many (not specifically Christian) situations. (He did in fact write a play, called, I think, *The Special Messenger* which was successfuly produced in Bristol. Unhappily I was unable to see it.)

Bill Purcell undertook to write an article for *Church Illustrated* emphasising the great possibilities of young people's service to the old.

C. A. Joyce emphasised characteristically that every Christian should be more personally self-giving, even if it only meant being a good listener or offering a shoulder to cry on.

Looking back on those ripples I think we were a small part of a general movement in the Church. In reading the books that were published only fifteen years or so ago it is quite astonishing to see how the emphasis in presenting the Christian gospel has changed. (In some ways, I think, it has swung too far towards more do-gooding and has excluded the supernatural and the whole background of eternity against which we live.) Charlie Moule, in a famous sermon preached in Cambridge only a few years ago, put the matter succinctly and admirably when he said, "When I was an undergraduate the underlying message was 'Come to Jesus'; today it is 'Give to Oxfam'."

Gerald Whitmarsh

At the second of these conferences (in early 1960) I met Gerald Whitmarsh, a devoted Christian, a lay reader, a skilled financier and a most attractive personality. I asked him, within minutes of our first meeting, whether he would act as my accountant and business manager. To my joy and great relief (for money bothers me) he agreed, in spite of all he had to do both in and out of the Church (he was chairman of Devon county council for five years, and chairman and director of several companies, apart from giving a great deal of time to the Church Board of Finance). He has become one of my best and most trusted friends and still manages my business and financial affairs. In years of prosperity he used to remind me that I was a high income man but never, because of tax and surtax, a rich man. This saved me from extravagance and the desire to give more generously than I could really afford.

Martin Willson

In 1960 I formed one of a broadcasting panel answering questions about the Christian faith from a girls' school just south of Bruton. Alan Gibson was in the chair and among the panellists was that vivacious and amusing personality, Miss Yanovsky. This was the first time I had met Penry Jones who was doing such splendid work for "the other channel". Some years later he became the B.B.C.'s head of religious broadcasting – a wise appointment in my opinion.

In March of the same year I broadcast from Sherborne School for Girls – probably more of a strain for Jennifer, then a pupil, than for me. This was one of the last times I saw Martin Willson, for he died suddenly of a heart attack in July. I felt a bit numb at first as I think many people did; the feeling of personal loss did not appear immediately. One didn't perhaps realise quite how deeply one cared for Martin, but there was a sense – a very real sense I think – that Martin's work was completed. He'd fought his fight, he'd done his job and he was now promoted as I believe into a higher field of action.

In the studio he was something of a perfectionist. If he felt that one could do it better, he wouldn't hesitate to say, in a kindly way, "Well now, Jack, try that again will you," or "Try that from this point again," until in the end he'd got the best out of you.

I had the rather melancholy honour of conducting a memorial service for him in St. Paul's church, Bristol on the 14th of July. The then Bishop of Crediton gave a glowing and hope-filled address, while the lesson was read by that well known broadcaster, Frank Gillard. The music was the responsibility of the B.B.C. West of England Singers, and since they all knew and loved Martin they gave of their quite splendid best. Many of the Limpley Stokers were able to be present at this service, and afterwards at a very informal meeting we decided not to hold the proposed further meeting. I think we were all deeply stricken by Martin's death and he had really been the heart and mind of the enterprise.

The New English Bible

1961 was a memorable year: it saw the publication of the New English Bible (or at least the New Testament), an event for which literally millions had been waiting. I was honoured to be asked to review it for the *Church Times,* and with a due sense of occasion Vera and I booked a suite at a very expensive hotel in Dartmoor. Within a week we found we had written some 8,000 words – far too long for a *Church Times* article. We decided that, on balance, the fourteen years of effort made by the translating panel had been well worthwhile and because it could not fail to speak to many modern people we could fairly claim that it was like a "sword unsheathed", and this became the title of the article.

Nevertheless we could not be blind to many of its faults, faults which we listed under the headings of Questionable Translation, Infelicities, Archaisms, Colloquialisms, Translator's English, and, to be fair, Felicities. Since my article, or any reprint of it is not today available, it will perhaps be interesting to give some examples under each heading.

I really cannot understand all these blemishes, and even errors, escaping the eagle eyes of more than a dozen high-calibre Greek scholars. "Homer," as I wrote in my article, "may nod, and be quickly forgiven, but where there is a posse of Homers, especially commissioned to keep one another on the alert, there should be no failure in style or in accuracy." There are nearly 200 of these serious failures.

Questionable Translation

In Mark 7:29 Jesus speaks to the Syrophoenician woman and is made to say, "For saying that you may go home content." Why content? The Greek word is *hupage*, a word of dismissal, used by Jesus to dismiss Satan in Matthew 4:10.

In John 8:42 the Jews protest at his accusation that their father was the devil "We are not base-born." This is by several centuries out of date, and I am not sure that it is accurate. The Greek word *porneia* surely means bastard or illegitimate rather than of humble birth.

In 1 John 2:2 we read, "He is himself the remedy for the defilement of our sins." Now you don't have a *remedy* for a *defilement*; you use soap and water, Vim, or the latest detergent.

Infelicities

In the parable of the wise and foolish virgins, in Matthew 25, we find the wise virgins refusing to share their oil in the style of a junior office-girl, remarking, "There will never be enough for us both." This importation of the lower-class usage of "never" for "not" is wildly out of place here.

In John 2:25 we read of Jesus that "He knew men so well, all of them, that he needed no evidence from others about a man for he himself could tell what was in a man." How clumsy can you get? The Authorised Version is clearer and more accurate.

Archaisms

In Matthew 25:12 we come across, "I declare, I do not know you." Where are we now – in Jane Austen's drawing room?

In 2 Timothy 2:18 we read, "They have shot wide of the truth in saying that our resurrection has already taken place." "They have shot wide of the truth" is *not* current English. "They are very wide of the mark in saying . . ." is still contemporary English. Did the translators read *no* modern novels, articles or even magazines?

Translator's English

Under this heading we noted, among several others, the New English Bible's version of 1 Timothy 6:18, "Tell them to hoard a wealth of noble actions by doing good," which was never current English in any century. But the prize really goes to the rendering of part of James 1:4 with the words, "If you give fortitude full play you will go on to complete a balanced character that will fall short in nothing." Really!

But there are certainly *Felicities*: "Be ye perfect as your father in Heaven is perfect" (Matt. 5:48) is almost impossible to translate. But the New English Bible panel comes up with "You must therefore be all goodness, just as your heavenly Father is all good." This is perfectly intelligible and implies an understandable process instead of an instant and impossible command. And in James 1:20 the translation "For a man's anger cannot promote the justice of God" is a most happy rendering.

The crisis

I was still doing a fair measure of speaking in schools and churches until the late summer of 1961. And then, quite suddenly, my speaking, writing and communicating powers stopped. I was not in a panic but I was certainly alarmed, and when a few weeks' rest brought no improvement I cancelled all speaking engagements for the rest of the year. My physical health was good for a man of fifty-five but all vision, drive and energy had vanished almost overnight. Of course I consulted my doctor who, naturally enough, suggested a commonsense course of cutting down my activities and a reminder that I had probably been overdoing it for years. One doctor in Plymouth, whom I consulted at Gerald Whitmarsh's request, told me I was "scooped out". The future seemed very uncertain – and I could hardly help feeling that my career as a writer and speaker was possibly at an end. After much thought I felt it was only fair to release Margery, for she was yet young enough to get another job. I gave her a substantial gift, wrote her a glowing testimonial and made her some small provision in way of a pension.

Fortunately for me my wife managed to get some domestic help in the house about this time, and was thus set free to help me with essential correspondence. In a very short time Vera had taught herself shorthand (her own version) and it was not long before she could type fast and accurately. Naturally I was grateful for this, but the latter part of 1961 is a dark and sad patch in my memory. With the sudden cut-off of creativity had also come a complete non-appreciation of colour or beauty in music, or indeed, in any form of art. It was a miserable monochrome world and my only work was the taking of a few services (hard labour instead of delight) and the answering of the letters which never stopped.

However, though still working in some darkness, I was able, early in 1962, to resume the translation of *Four Prophets*, which I had started the previous year. I found I got on much more quickly with Vera as my secretary and I cannot give too much praise to Edwin Robertson. Although one of the busiest of men I have ever met, he was always ready to be consulted by letter or telephone.

C.C.L.

Some time in 1961 I had founded a small private non-profit-making company called Christian Communications Ltd. This concerned itself not with the big causes, it was too small for that, but with individual cases of men or women (mostly abroad) who needed some piece of equipment such as a tape-recorder, a film projector or even something so prosaic as a duplicator. We made our gifts to people who were personally known to us, and for some thirteen years were able to meet the needs of a wide variety of Christian people. The funds were provided by some of my own writing and the whole thing was on a small scale. But we derived a lot of satisfaction from being able to step in when the individual, the society, the church or the school could not provide financially for an essential need. I think the biggest gifts we ever made were to Salisbury theological college and to the Diocese of Exeter. We provided each of them with a television camera, a video-tape recorder and, of course, a monitor screen. The young men at Salisbury, with a great deal of labour, converted a disused cellar into a studio. I remember visiting this and learning, as indeed I had anticipated, what a useful tool this apparatus was for those who were learning the art of public communication.

Eventually, because of the distance and the difficulty of meeting, we decided to merge C.C.L.'s activities with the large worldwide organisation called the World Association for Christian Communication, for which Edwin Robertson had put in several years and many thousands of miles of devoted service. It was later administered by the Christian Broadcasting Commission.

14

Light at the End of the Tunnel

There are diseases of the body which produce depression of mind, a phenomenon which many of us have experienced after recovering from influenza or some other virus infection. The colour, the meaning and the point of life simply disappears for a time. We pray apparently to an empty heaven, and in our misery we torture ourselves by brutal self-condemnation. There are however those who have to endure such conditions month after month, and even year after year. We who know something of God's love can truly help them by our love and our prayers. There *is* light at the end of their dark tunnel. In the meantime we may help them far more by our encouragement than perhaps we know.

This chapter, I must confess, I write after a lot of hesitation and even after making up my mind to write it I do so with considerable reluctance. This is not because I am any more shy than the next man at admitting my own weaknesses or of having to set down that I have often met the frightening experiences that have come to me over recent years with terror, bewilderment, occasional lack of courage and even the sense that the faith on which I base my life is threatened and shaken. And I am quite sure this reluctance is not based on fear that such self-revelation might destroy any image which my writings or broadcasts may have established. I have never claimed to be more than a learner in the Christian Way, and I have never sought to minimise the difficulties and dangers that always beset the path of following Christ. I think my unwillingness to write about these experiences is because I do not want such accounts to carry a flavour of self-pity, defeatism or utter despair.

Depression

A severe blow fell in the very early 1960s (as I have explained in the previous chapter under the heading of *The Crisis*) which has affected my life ever since. Without any particular warning the springs of creativity were suddenly dried up; the ability to communicate disappeared overnight and it looked as if my career as a writer and translator was over. I know now, but had no idea then, that this was the first inkling of a condition known to the medical and psychiatric world as a depression, a condition which was to be with me for several years.

I had never heard of the word depression being used in a technical sense and did not know there was such a thing. I took a few days off, cancelled a few future engagements and tried to take things easy. But it didn't work; the feeling of being utterly drained of all emotion and desire persisted and I simply ceased to work. Naturally I thought there must be some physical cause for this, especially as I was beginning to get those unpleasant headaches and pains in the eyes which have been my companions for so long now. I visited various consultants to see if I had, as I suspected, any sinus trouble; I had my heart thoroughly tested and even my brain-waves spelt out on a machine. But nobody could find anything physically wrong.

After a few months, during which I was not entirely idle, I found the mental pain more than I felt I could bear and I went as a voluntary patient to a psychiatric clinic not far from here. This was the point of breakdown, and after much hard thinking I have decided to write down my experience. My reason for writing this chapter is that it may help someone else who is depressed and in mental pain. It may help simply to know that one whom the world would regard as successful and whose worldly needs are comfortably met can still enter this particular hell, and have to endure it for quite a long time.

A ray of light

Then there came something of a remission, for under the kindly encouragement of Edwin Robertson I was persuaded to translate into modern English the Old Testament prophets, Amos, Hosea, Micah and First-Isaiah. My knowledge of Hebrew was not very great but Edwin put all his expert knowledge at my disposal, and temporarily the will and the ability to communicate returned.

Why translate the Old Testament?

I suppose the primary reason for agreeing to cope with the difficult Hebrew of the Old Testament was that people kept asking me to do so. Many who felt that I had helped them to understand the New Testament implored me to do the same thing for them with the Old. I replied to them all, and said that the problem was a complicated one. What could be done with the comparatively workaday Greek of the New Testament could not be done with the craggy grandeur of Old Testament Hebrew.

Yet people still asked me, and in the end I began to feel that I must make the attempt. Once I had begun the task I became appalled at the difficulty. But there was no escape, no Hebrew without tears. And yet, such is human pride, I also felt challenged. I had put my hand to the plough, and I must finish the furrow. Fortunately I had good friends to help and some excellent commentaries to consult, and Vera as my secretary. Yet there were a good many times in the two years I gave to the work when I wondered whether I should ever make a decent job of it – or even finish it at all. But thanks to the encouragement of my friends and never forgetting the grace of God the work was finally done.

The reason why I chose the work of these four prophets is something like this: I felt that the purely narrative parts of the Old Testament are reasonably clear and do not cry out for translation into modern language; I did not wish to touch the poetic beauty of the Psalms; and I felt that here at this critical stage of the history of God's chosen people four very different men were inspired to see and speak the truth that lies behind the superficiality of history. This eighth century B.C. was a momentous time in the history of the world. Rome was little more than a village; the great days of Greek culture were yet to come. The tiny nation of God's choosing was sandwiched between the great powers of Assyria and Egypt. Outwardly it had never been so affluent, but inwardly, as each of these prophets fearlessly declares, it was suffering terrible spiritual degeneration. The warnings in the four books, terrible as they sound in our ears, were meant to awaken men from their dreams and make them face reality. All four prophets see utter catastrophe as the inevitable consequence of the nation's faithlessness towards God and worship of idols; but all four hold out the highest hopes if men will turn in true repentance to the true and living God.

I found a quality of remarkable spiritual strength in these men's writings. Despite the difficulties of translation and the strangeness of some of their imagery, I must record my firm impression that these men spoke as men inspired by the living God. There is divine authority behind their warnings and their promises.

For us today, living about 2,600 years later, this authority comes across with salutary force. We get the impression from some recent books that God only exists by kind permission of human beings. But here in the world of these men of God, the very opposite is true. God is the Creator, of infinite wisdom and power, and men are his creatures. It is his world not theirs, and if they are wise they will try to live according to his laws. This is surely a timely reminder for us today.

Again, all four of these prophets remind us that religion merely as religion is useless. Unless the worship of God is coupled with justice and compassion towards our fellow men it is an empty thing. This insistence on the close connection between love of God and love of man was, of course, emphasised again and again by Jesus Christ himself. But it is a truth that we need to be reminded of constantly.

I think we need to feel again the fire and beauty, yes even the pain and ferocity, of these four men who saw the truth so plainly that they had to speak it at whatever cost.

Relapse

Having completed this task I felt ready, temporarily as it happened, to accept the next challenge. But alas this was not to be. I can well remember sitting in the S.P.C.K. bookshop in Salisbury autographing copies of *Four Prophets* and being seized by an utterly irrational panic at the thought of meeting people whom I did not know. This mounted to such a pitch that by tea-time I was obliged to ask my wife to drive me home. It appeared to me then that I was not so much back to square one, but set back into all the nervousness and uncertainty of my early days in the ministry. This was a heavy blow, indeed, and I did not know at all how to cope with it. Fortunately for me I had no financial worries since I was earning a comfortable income, thanks to the expert help and guidance of my friend and accountant Gerald Whitmarsh. But that was not really the issue; the heart of the matter was that the very faith which I had striven to impart to others had now deserted me emotionally. I say emotionally deliberately for never in the dark days that were to follow did I ever doubt the reality of God.

Breakdown

I suppose I could be said to have suffered my fair share of the usual temptations of "the world, the flesh and the devil", but I am not talking of these here. What I am talking about is that fearful attack upon the central personality of a man, which indeed seems to threaten his very integrity and which in popular parlance is called a nervous breakdown or nervous collapse. I am not of course talking about actual mental disease or insanity, matters of which I know nothing, but of those intense pressures which build up, possibly for years, and result in the often quite unexpected collapse of a personality. I have found from conversation as well as from correspondence that this is yet another of those forbidden subjects about which a tactful curtain of silence has for many years been drawn. Even today with all the advances in medical and psychiatric treatment there is a vast amount of ignorance even among the so-called experts. Such an attack or series of attacks might last for weeks, months or even years and then vanish without trace. I can only testify to the fact that it would have been of inestimable comfort and encouragement to me in some of my darkest hours if I could have come across even one book written by someone who had experienced and survived the hellish torments of mind which can be produced. And, alas, I know very very few clergy or ministers who would even know what the sufferer was talking about. That is why I decided, however reluctantly, that this chapter must be written by someone who has experienced the almost unendurable sense of terror and alienation.

Of course it is more than possible that most of my readers will never experience this particular Hell which life can inflict upon human beings. In that case, I beg you not to be unmindful of the unseen and often inexpressible sufferings of others. At least do not look down on those who are undergoing what seem to you to be purely imaginary terrors. And please have the charity to remember that most of them are fighting a battle of almost unbelievable ferocity just to keep going at all.

It can happen to anyone

Until my own experience I had little idea how widespread such personal afflictions can be. But in the last few years, I have been compelled to realise that a breakdown or depression is a very common thing. Obviously there are some catastrophes and disasters which afflict any man and can cause him, at least temporarily, to try to withdraw from life. But the recuperative powers of nature will almost always heal him. But what continues to astonish me is that such breakdowns may occur without any obvious precipitatory cause. Moreover, they can happen to the highly intelligent or the relatively ignorant. I have known and talked to such diverse people as a bus driver, a music teacher, a highly skilled accountant, a priest, a B.B.C. commentator, a brilliant musician, a farmer, a water-engineer, a C.I.D. detective, a brilliant and successful publisher, and many more of widely differing ages who suffered in varying degrees and different forms the agonies of such an attack upon the personality.

Freedom to talk

In the clinic I found that many of those who were suffering, or were emerging from, this depression extremely ready to talk as soon as they realised that I knew at first-hand the sort of things they were enduring. Many were almost pathetically grateful to have their terrors and tensions expressed in articulate terms. For many people, however skilled in their particular callings, find it hard to analyse, and even more difficult to express in words, what appears to be destroying them from inside. I do not myself believe that there is any substitute for the long unhurried conversations between the sufferer and the compassionate trained psychiatrist. In the clinic which I attended you were lucky if you got ten minutes or a quarter of an hour's direct talk with the man who was trained to help you, *per week*! It was nobody's fault of course for all the staff were busy. Despite the use of drugs, which did me no good at all, there really can be no substitute for the healing of the mind by the encouragement and understanding of one who knows what he is talking about.

The staff were kindness itself, but as far as I was concerned the daily contact with others who were suffering as I was did me more good than anything.

Mental pain

The hardest thing of all to bear is what I can only describe as a nameless mental pain, which is, as far as I know, beyond the reach of any drug, and which I have tried in vain to describe to anyone. Other patients at the clinic knew it in varying degrees and bore it stoically. But it is so overwhelming that one can understand the temptation to suicide. One of the psychiatrists asked me to write down, as far as I could, the nature of the almost intolerable pain. He was a distinguished man in his field and was about to visit a number of mental hospitals in a south London group. He told me afterwards that the psychiatrists and nurses agreed that my statement represented a pain which many of their patients suffered from but were not articulate enough to put into words.

I wrote:

When this utterly overwhelming pain occurs it seems to me to be due to the simultaneous occurrence of the following four trains of thought. (Each by itself is nearly intolerable, but when all four attack together the unhappy self feels utterly overwhelmed.)

(a) *Diminution of the personality.* This is a slow but inevitable diminution of the self and it is apparently leading to its final extinction. All sorts of images of erosion may occur but they all point to one end: the final destruction of the personality. This is not a fear of death but a fear of being diminished to vanishing point so that one ceases to be anything at all.

(b) *Alienation.* This feeling can occur in a number of ways. Familiar things become somehow touched with horror; beauty in word or music is discordant, even though some small part of oneself tries to reassure one that there is really beauty there. The sense of alienation means that one is not in one's own country, or has strayed into a strange country by mistake. Thus words have no meaning (as if a different language were spoken here): money has no value (as if an entirely different currency were in force). Everything is out of joint as though some sort of cosmic jerk had altered the very nature of things.

(c) *Self-condemnation.* This is no rational weighing up of one's personal value. It is a roaring galloping torrent of condemnation directed against the self's achievements. With remorseless energy this particular "demon" rushes to and fro and up and down in one's mind, and with savage cruelty exposes everything that the self has done as being useless and worthless.

(d) *Agony by comparison.* The effect of this "demon" is clearly an ally of the preceding one. But instead of reducing achievements to nothing it compares the prisoner's present miserable state with joyful states he has known before but which are utterly beyond his reach. If the memory is full (and it often is in this abnormal state) this is quite a long business. And since the most miserable of men usually has some streak of hope left in him he lets the process go on, hoping for some encouragement. But he is given instead an agony of comparison – the excruciating difference between his present condition and that which he enjoyed for many years. He may not, at any rate at first, be able to stop this fury of self-denigration but in time he may be able to see that it is irrational and learn firmly to switch it off.

These four violent emotional torments when they happen together are enough to daunt the bravest. But they too, like all the other disorientated emotions, will always pass. They can last for a few minutes to several hours or even years and they are fatiguing and dispiriting. We can, I think, learn to pay less and less attention to them. For myself I know nothing that can be relied upon to jerk the mind back into seeing sense though I know of others who are greatly helped by anti-depressant drugs.

The process of recovery

One of the most ridiculous, yet painful, features of these depressive states is the sudden eruption of irrational fear and nameless panic. I have never been able to say what triggers them off, if indeed they are so triggered. It seems to be part of the mental illness. The best thing to do is to let them evaporate off, leaving sensible reality behind. But I have to admit that they are embarrassing and humiliating, for fears that one has conquered a hundred times, even the fears of childhood re-appear with monstrous force. But if we can learn with Alice to say "You're nothing but a pack of cards!" we have taken at least a step forward. The worst thing is to allow oneself to be afraid of the fear of fears. They are not in any way real, however alarming they feel at the time. They perish, sooner or later, by our deliberate neglect of them.

The process of recovery is sometimes very short and sometimes very long, but it is a *process*. We don't know (nor I believe does the cleverest psychiatrist) what is happening in our bewildered and sometimes frightened minds. But as the body automatically, given a reasonable chance, heals itself so does the mind. Skilled help may be needed on certain points of the road, and the steadfast companionship of a friend (or better still a loving wife who does not fuss).

A deeper trust in God

And where, you may well ask, does the Christian faith come into all this? The answer is that probably emotionally it is of little help at all. It is only at the very centre of our being that, despite any negative or evil attack, we can rest on the eternal and unchanging God. We may well have to learn to trust this living God without any comforting feeling whatever, and this is no easy lesson to learn. In fact it seems to me that, for the Christian anyway, the undoubted evil of this form of suffering can be turned into good by learning a deeper trust in the real and living God. It may be that we have relied too much upon our own abilities, our own emotional security or upon the props of true and earthly friends. But in this painful experience we are stripped of our pride and pious imaginings. Temporarily at least we have no one who can understand what we are going through. We are alone in this bewildering world and our only hope is in God, not probably the God who has satisfied us in past years or the God whom we imagined for our comfort, but the Spirit behind all creation. It is to know more deeply this real true God that we are permitted to go through the pains and humiliations of mental pain. I do not write these words lightly or without thought, but to believe that there is a deeper purpose at work (which temporarily we can only see in glimpses of insight) helps enormously through what is bound to be a hard struggle.

Ring of truth

Broadcasts and books like *Honest to God* and *The Passover Plot* disturbed the faith of many during the sixties.

To walk by faith, which is what we have to do in this life, is never easy, and I decided that it might be helpful to others if I set down my own simple testimony. Encouraged by Edward England of Hodder & Stoughton, I did this and the book was published in 1967 as *Ring of Truth: A Translator's Testimony*. The response astonished me. I did not have one hostile letter and the book was welcomed by a very wide variety of people. I made a selection from some of these responses including them in the Author's Preface when the book was re-issued later in the year.

From a young Divinity student, quite unknown to me:

I too have been appalled by the way many of the "experts" have spoken publicly about their doubts and by their lack of discretion have destroyed or severely shaken the faith of many young Christians, some of whom are known to me.

Thank you for your courage in speaking out against such indiscretion, but thank you also for the remainder of the book which in a positive way acts as a very wonderful handbook to the New Testament, and a very stimulating and refreshing aid in meeting a real and living Christ through its pages.

And a group of students at a college in Scotland, not noted for ultra-conservatism:

Your spiritual discernment, coupled to a deep sense of humility, makes your thesis ring with notes of conviction and joy. At a time when the central truths of our faith are being subject to cynicism in every area of society . . . it gives tremendous encouragement to hear again the call of integrity, grounded in the triumph of Calvary . . .

But not only students. Here is a letter from a schoolmaster who teaches both religious instruction and biology:

Your recent book came into my hands at a most effective moment . . . I read to the class as much as could conveniently be covered in the period available. The reading commanded the attention and respect of these senior pupils, and has given valuable affirmation to the facts that I had put before them.

A young housewife, who some years ago was a member of my youth group, expressed what many felt in those troublesome days of the sixties:

Your new book has completely dispelled the anguish I felt when I read *Honest to God* and which lurked at the back of my mind for several years. That book caused me to kneel in tears on Easter Evening after a particularly beautiful service, and wonder if all I had believed and tried to follow for years was in vain.

I began to hear from the "dignitaries", bishops and professors of theology, but not only experts in divinity. Here is one from a leading expert in the field of psychiatry:

I read it through at a sitting . . . and thought that, once again, you had demonstrated that unique capacity of yours for stating the experiences which many of us have in our religion and making clear to us the roots of our faith and why we are justified in preserving these in our simple, traditional way.

One typical extract:

Last year, just before Easter, I read *The Passover Plot* and it really upset me. I attended Easter services but wondering all the time if there were any sense in it. After reading your book – twice over – I feel happy again.

These are only a few of a constant stream of letters. They confirm in my own mind the strong impression that, while we may well have to alter our language, our methods and our presentation of the everlasting gospel, the Christian faith is rooted in history, and the living Spirit of God is as alive and powerful as ever.

Personal correspondence
Apart from the letters of unknown correspondents, I wrote to several eminent men who appeared to have passed through a similar experience to my own, of depression and breakdown. They must, of course, remain anonymous. One was an enormous help to me. About the time that *Ring of Truth* was published – in 1967 – he wrote, pouring out his own story and it awakened an immediate sympathy. Towards the end of one of his letters, he encouraged me greatly:

Well, my dear J.B., I don't know why I am tipping all this out on you. It may not be the least use . . . but my heart goes out to you, because in some ways we seem to have been in the same dark valley. We *shall* emerge and we *shall* triumph, I am sure of that, if we endure to the end and soldier on as you say . . .

And then the final word,

Whatever happens in your mind you have wrought a mighty work for the kingdom of God. No one in your generation has done more. God bless you. You will find the way through and so shall I. May it be soon!

This letter was an enormous help, because I had always admired the writer and his outpourings had put him up in my estimation by several hundred per cent! There was a great deal of similarity in our experience of life.

Much earlier, the late Leonard Browne had very easily and skilfully helped me to see that I was trying to please an exacting father. My life's drive, although I did not know it at the time, was to become so wonderful that I was beyond all criticism. The lack of love and security had to be compensated for by performance. Leonard Browne used to tell me that I was trying to reach 130%, and that the neurotic symptoms were a protection against this.

For twenty years – say from 1935 to 1955 – with the help of a most understanding wife who is quite the best human being I have ever met, I thought I had got the whole thing beaten. I was not prepared for the resurgence of the old fantastic image of myself under the stimulus of enormous popularity and success.

The hidden God

It was in this personal correspondence with men who had passed through the same dark valley and had known comparable success that I could most easily share my experiences. I quote from a letter I wrote to one such on 19th February, 1967:

Then quite suddenly the creative urge had gone and the colour and meaning had drained out of life. It seemed to me as though everything was being knocked out of my hands. My capacity for affection almost completely disappeared and, worst of all, I lost all sense of God. I don't think I ever seriously thought I had a "hot line to Heaven", but there was always a definite someone (quite distinct from the father image) to whom I could turn, and who was often consciously with me.

This loss of all sense of God led to a situation of acute anxiety. Being fairly suddenly deprived of the ability to "perform", my sense of security and of being useful deserted me and all kinds of nameless terrors swept over me, usually at night . . . I knew perfectly well why I felt insecure and afraid, but I could not see what I could do about it. No psychiatrist could tell me anything that I did not know already and the psychotropic drugs did not seem to suit me, even in tiny doses. So I set myself down for what must be a long siege and so it has proved . . . The drive to be successful now went into reverse in a most frightening way. A great deal of my time, waking and sleeping, became one violent condemnation of myself.

I think, to be frank, that I can see the hand of God in all this. There will certainly be no VIPs in heaven and I think I can accept the fact that I am basically a perfectly ordinary person. To be made to realise this is terribly painful because the unconscious is thoroughly amoral and is determined to defend the *status quo* to the last. I don't think God minds hurting us, but I am absolutely certain he will never harm us. It may even be the assaults of the "principalities and powers" who seem to be allowed to pick their targets. I simply do not know. But I am improving slowly and I have gained much greater insights than I had in the days of health and prosperity.

Harry Williams

A book by Harry Williams, *The True Wilderness* and subsequent correspondence with him helped me greatly. I think the reason was that he put forward the suggestion that Jesus himself faced agonies and evils both at the Temptations and in the Garden of Gethsemane, that he was not rescued, but was given the strength to go through with it. Although I know no details I gather that Harry Williams has been through what he calls, "sheer bloody hell". When he wrote, he offered me no pious platitude, but the strong encouragement of knowing that Christ went through something of this darkness himself – although, of course, I know that it was infinitely deeper in quality.

Harry Williams also suggested to me that when the experiences are really evil, and they sometimes are terrifyingly so, we may fairly consider that we are sharing something of Christ's agony for the world. He further made the common-sense suggestion that the people who are "most used of God" frequently pay a very high price for it in personal suffering.

Acceptance

In the meantime – for frequently we have to continue living and working – the best practical solution seems to be to sit down and reckon up what we can, and cannot do. It is of no use cursing ourselves (or fate, or God) because we are handicapped. Let us accept this mental or nervous pain as if it were a physical illness. Let us not waste time in endless self-probing and attempts to understand what is going on. God is in this process, and he who made the human mind understands its strange workings, we may be sure. So, with or without any religious feeling, let us go on praying, hoping and doing what we can. We may get complete remissions when all the nervous symptoms disappear and we wonder what on earth all the fuss was about. We can be truly thankful for these and regard them as tokens of recovery. We may get sudden relapses which can feel quite devastating. But they are not real, and must be endured without self-pity until they pass. All the recoveries that I have known have a pattern of ebb and flow. But if the real inward self is committed to God the direction is onward and upward, however battered we feel at times.

As far as I am concerned my affliction, which lasted on and off for a long time, was rarely so bad that I could not work at all. But I had to change my own attitude towards what I was trying to do. I had done enough rushing about speaking, preaching and lecturing, and I must give more time to reflection on what I believed and proclaimed.

Commentaries

In September 1968, Edwin Robertson wrote to me suggesting a series of commentaries based on N.T.I.M.E., similar to what Mowbrays were then publishing in relation to the Jerusalem Bible and what had been done for Moffat many years ago. I had had the same idea in mind for many years, but I kept telling people that I was a communicator rather than a scholar. I was not a little doubtful of the value of my translation if it were microscopically examined by an over-zealous commentator. The original object of the exercise was to make the New Testament relevant and meaningful and be blowed to the minutiae of scholarship. My passion remained to remove obscurities and explain in simple terms what every scholar knows. But about that time I was receiving letters from people teaching the New Testament in schools who asked for advice on commentaries, and I was beginning to see the need for what I can only describe as a non-technical commentary. All I could find were too expert for the average reader. I was coming to the conclusion that the hungry sheep needed sensible orthodoxy more than some of our leaders seemed to suppose.

Our work on *Four Prophets* had given me enough confidence in Edwin Robertson to suggest that he be the general editor of this series of commentaries. He felt I should share the task with him. But my health made it impossible for me to be sure that I could take the responsibility. It was a great relief to be assured by him that he would shoulder the burden when I couldn't.

As the work proceeded it became increasingly clear that I should have to revise my translation and I did not see how I would find the strength to do this.

The commentary on Mark

It was at first suggested that I should do the commentary on Colossians and two other epistles because *Letters to Young Churches* started with Colossians. But the commentator due to do *Mark* fell by the wayside and so I took that on. It was eventually published as *Peter's Portrait of Jesus* by Collins in 1976. The experience of writing a commentary set me free to say a number of things that one couldn't really hint at in a translation. I personally dislike footnotes and have almost entirely avoided them. And I don't think it's altogether right to put any twist or slant into the words used in translation to indicate what your own convictions may be about a particular passage. The commentary I wrote was deliberately simple and uncomplicated. I kept in mind a study group of men who were reading the New Testament books with me and each other.

I think we clergy are constantly tempted to forget how very ignorant the ordinary members of our study groups are over the New Testament itself. They may, for example, be excellent craftsmen, first-class scientists or very able executives. But they have never found time to learn the barest outlines of the New Testament documents. They are in these biblical matters as much babes in arms as I would be, for instance, in accountancy or in a science laboratory. I had no doubt that scholars would condemn my commentary as being much over-simplified. But I didn't really mind about that as long as the ordinary man without special training could be interested and even fascinated by what is after all part of the Word of God.

Revising a classic

Towards the end of 1969 and through much of 1970 an essential task was revising the *New Testament in Modern English*. Because the first of the commentaries was to be Edwin's "Corinthians", I started by revising that. Vera and I were both struck by a miserable flu, but before succumbing we did manage to finish 1 Corinthians before Christmas. There were quite a lot of small errors – not terribly important – but now was the chance to make the translation as accurate as we could. They were sent to the publisher so that the new text could be used in the commentary. Then, purely as a matter of interest, despite our assorted aches and pains, we revised the first chapter of Mark. There was absolutely nothing to correct. I soon found this to be the general case. The gospels were straightforward. It was only in some of Paul's labyrinthine arguments and his occasionally cavalier treatment of the Greek language where revision became a time-consuming business. But it was done.

What was eventually published as a completely revised edition in 1972 was in fact a new translation from the latest and best Greek text published by the United Bible Societies in 1966. Naturally, some considerable part of the former translation reappeared, but that was because after considerable thought I could not improve upon the wording. However, every single Greek word was read and considered. This exacting task took me two years in the ebb and flow of my depression which never totally left me for more than a short period.

Sharing the problem of suffering

I continued to receive many letters, some from fellow sufferers. To one such I wrote:

> I think prolonged suffering whether it is mental, physical or both, tends to make us impatient, resentful, angry and frustrated; we begin to see the jaws of despair. The only value I can see in these experiences is that they do give us more insight and sympathy with the sufferings of others. I never thought, for example, that I should ever know the type of despair that leads people to self-destruction. I know it now, but I am still firmly of the belief that it really solves nothing and is a cowardly gesture.
>
> I think the frightful thing about continual suffering is that it takes the colour and joy out of almost all the proper pleasures of living. It also, in my case, except for rare intervals, tends to destroy the sense of God. It is no use comparing afflictions; my pains are not your pains or any-one else's. To me it calls for all my inward courage and all my faith in the living God to survive at all. It is really much

more than a crumb of comfort to know that whatever we feel God knows all about it. Even when we find it next to impossible to pray I am basically convinced that He understands this too.

There is an almost inescapable loneliness about the experience of prolonged suffering. If we hang on, and of course we must, I am pretty certain that we shall emerge with a far more robust faith. I haven't even begun to "welcome" my afflictions, as St. James suggests in his epistle, but men and women have learned to do this and it must be possible.

Doing battle against the Evil One

Christ made no promise that those who followed him in his plan of re-establishing life on its proper basic principles would enjoy special immunity from pain and sorrow – nor did he himself experience such immunity. He did, however, promise enough joy and courage, enough love and confidence in God to enable those who went his way to do far more than survive. Because they would be in harmony with the very Life and Spirit of God they would be able to defeat evil. They would be able to take the initiative and destroy evil with good.

Christ definitely spoke of a power of spiritual evil, and, using the language of his contemporaries, he called this power "Satan", the "Devil", or the "Evil One". Now whatever mystery lies behind the existence of such an evil power – whether we accept a Miltonic idea of a fallen angelic power or whether we conceive the evil spirit in the world as arising out of the cumulative effects of centuries of selfish living – there can be no blinking the fact that Christ spoke, and acted, on the assumption that there is a power of evil operating in the world. If we accept his claim to be God this must make us think seriously.

We are so accustomed in modern thought to regard evil as error, as the growing pains of civilisation, or simply as an inexplicable problem, that the mind does not readily accept what is in effect God's own explanation – that there is a spirit of evil operating in the world. We find Christ speaking quite plainly of this spirit as responsible for disease and insanity as well as being the unremitting enemy of those who want to follow the new, true order.

There are times when skies are overcast, when spiritual things seem to have lost their meaning and God himself appears to be far away. This is where we are to do battle, to go on actively, and even aggressively, believing in the goodness and purpose of God; never mind what happens or what we feel.

Sometimes again we make progress, at other times we seem to do no more than maintain our footing. But the practised Christian soldier can at least do this. Paul says, "Even when you have fought to a standstill you may still stand your ground."

And all the trumpets sounded

In my opinion whatever we may have to go through now is less than nothing compared with the magnificent future God has in store for us. The whole creation is on tiptoe to see the wonderful sight of the sons of God coming into their own. The world of creation cannot see as yet reality, not because it chooses to be blind, but because in God's purpose it has been so limited – yet it has been given hope. And the hope is that in the end the whole of created life will be rescued from the tyranny of change and decay, and have its share in that magnificent liberty which can only belong to the children of God!

J.B. Phillips died at home in Swanage, 21st July 1982, after prolonged illness.

Index

Acts of the Apostles, 154, 159–60; sermons from, 126
air raids: World War I, 30, 38–9; II, 87, 88–90, 91–3, 95–9, 102–3
alcohol and teetotalism, 162–3
Alfriston, Sussex, 86
Alice (maid), 31
alienation, sense of, 203
Amos (prophet), 198, 199
Anerley, London, 72, 76, 78
Appleyard, Dr. and Mrs., 185
Arnold, Malcolm, 15–16
Australia, letters from, 161, 165–6, 168
Australian Broadcasting Company, 115–16, 161
authors, request advice, 170–1
Axminster, Devon, 180

ballet, 83–4
balloons, barrage, 88, 98; used to clean roofs, 120
Bangor, summer school, 118
Barnes, Sir George, 116
Barnes, London, 11, 21–4, 26–8
Battle of Britain, 88–90, 91–3, 95–9, 102–3
Beaton, Cecil, self-portrait, 58
Bell, Dr. G.K.A., 174
Bennett, R. G., 103, 121–2
Bentwaters, Suffolk, U.S.A.F., 175–7, 182
Bible: Old Testament, 198–9; see also New Testament and names of books
Black, Professor George P., 165
Blackheath, London, 80–7
Bles, Geoffrey (publisher), 107–8, 157; offices, 158, 182

boat race, Oxford/Cambridge, 18–19
Boddington, F., 122
Book of Common Prayer, 24–5, 174
Bornet, Philip, 121
Bournemouth, 155, 186; Branksome, 33, 36
Bowles, Frank, 103–4
Branksome, nr. Bournemouth, 33, 36
Brazil, letter from, 166
Brett, George, 183
Bristol, B.B.C., 160–1
British Broadcasting Corporation: audition for, 114; Bristol, 160–1; 'Christian Forum', 180, 181; overseas service, 125; plays on life of Jesus, 177–8; religious broadcasting dept., 114–16; Scottish Home Service, 179; services broadcast, 114, 125; speeches from Acts, 126; suggestions to, 188, 189; television, 161
British Oxygen Company, 120
Brown, Guy, 128–9, 182, 183, 184, 186, 187
Brown, Karl, 185
Browne, Leonard (psychiatrist), 77, 83, 208

Cambridge: Emmanuel College, 51–3, 55–8, 60–1, 62, 173; Holy Trinity Church, 55; Ridley Hall, 64–6
Cambridge Intercollegiate Christian Union, 52–3, 55, 56
caricatures, drawing, 57–8
Catford School, London, 91

Charles (Uncle), 22–3
Chesterton, G.K., 57
Chichester, Sussex, 174–5
Children's Encyclopedia, 32
Children's Special Service Mission,
 61
Christian Broadcasting
 Commission, 195
Christian Church, early, 159–60
Christian Communications Ltd,
 194–5
Christian Forum broadcasts, 180–1
Christmas, 34, 154
Church Missionary Society, 171
church roofs, cleaning, 120
Church Times, 191
Collins (publishers), 157
Colossians, Letter of Paul to the, 100
commentaries, 211–12
Compton, Fay, 177, 178
copper-plate writing, 27
copyright, 171
Corinthians, Letters of Paul to the,
 147–8, 212–13
Culdrose, Cornwall, 180, 181
Currie, James and Peggy, 179

Davis, Joan, 138
de la Tour de Berry, Rev. Oscar, 162
de Mille, Cecil B., 138
de Pemberton, Roger, 78
Dean, Maurice, 115
death, encounters with, 35–6, 37,
 73–4
depression, 193–4, 196–7, 200–4,
 207–11, 213–14; acceptance,
 210–11; process of recovery,
 204–5
Devonshire, 34, 54–5, 180
divorce, 86, 135
Dorking, mission, 156, 172

East Sheen, London, 29–31;
 Christ church, 34–5
Eastbourne, 71–2, 76, 77
Edinburgh, St. Giles Cathedral,
 179–80
electrical experiments, 46–50
Emanuel School, Wandsworth,
 36–7, 37–41, 43, 44, 45, 50–1, 56;

entrance exam, 33; dinner tickets,
 46–7
Emmanuel College *see* Cambridge
England, Edward, 205
English, for New Testament
 translation, 152–3
English Tripos, 60
Epistles, New Testament, 59, 94,
 99–100; to Colossians, 100; to
 Corinthians, 147–8, 212–13; to
 Romans, 143–4; to Timothy, 193
Eric (friend), 120
Essex, E.C., 65
Ethiopia, letter from, 167–8
Evans, Kenneth, 156
Evans, Rev. Louis H., 137
evil, power of, 214–15
Exeter, Devon, 180
extra-sensory perception (E.S.P.),
 71, 119, 120, 132–3

faith, 205–7
Falconer, Ronald, 115
Ford, Sidney, 67, 68
Forest Home conference centre,
 U.S.A., 130–2, 172
fundamentalism, 65, 144–7, 150

Gamages, catalogue, 43
gardening, 20–1
Gerson, Mark (photographer), 157–8
Ghana, letter from, 167
Gibb, Jocelyn, 157, 158
Gibbons, Stella, 157–8
Gibson, Alan, 180–1, 190
Gibson, Glen, 179
Gibson, Paul, 65
Gillingham, Canon F.H., 80–1,
 85–6, 87
Glasgow, 179
God: early belief in, 17–18; hidden,
 208–9; ideas of, 67, 111, 124, 199;
 Paul's idea of, 167; promise of,
 215; and suffering, 37, 113,
 208–9, 213–14; trust in, 205
Goodey, Frank, 121
Goodwin, Shirley, 39, 51
Graham, Dr. Billy, 116
Grandfather, 25, 33
Granta, 57–8

Greek: studied at school, 50, 51; at Cambridge, 57; of New Testament, 141, 152; request for help with, 165–6; translated, 122–4
Green, Sister Marjorie, 95
Greenwood, L.G.H. (tutor), 52, 57, 63, 173
Groves, Amy, 161
Guiseley, Yorks, 85

Harrott, Mr. (verger), 90
healing, and prayer, 70, 112–14
Hembry, Basil, 188
Henderson, Rev. Kenneth, 115–16,
Hewitt, Canon Gordon, 125
Highway Press, 171
Hills, Rev. Leslie, 87
Hither Green cemetery, London, 87, 91–2, 97
Hodder & Stoughton (publishers), 172, 205
holidays, childhood, 33–4
Hollywood, 130, 132, 136–9
honeymoon, 86
Hopkins, Margery, 117, 128, 133, 140, 154, 156, 194
Hosea (prophet), 198, 199
hospital visiting, 118–19
Hulbert, Dr. H. H., 66
Hurn airport, 175, 176–7
hymns, 26

Ile de France (liner), 139
Indian Head, U.S.A., 185
Isaiah (prophet), 198–9

James, Letter of, 193
James, Marguerite, 136, 162–3
James, Dr. Walt, 129–30, 136, 162–3
Japan, letter from, 148–9
Joel, Mr. (architect), 127
John, First Letter of, 192
John, Gospel According to, 192–3
Jones, Penry, 190–1
Jones, Vera *see* Phillips, Vera
Joyce, C.A., 188, 189–90

Kaye, Danny, 138–9

Kennedy-Bell, Rev. W.D., 115, 117, 125
Keswick Convention, 56, 61
King's Own youth club, Lee, 99–100
Knox, Ronald, 151

Lanford, Con, 182
Langdon, Canon W., 154
Lake Tahoe, U.S.A., 135–6, 172
Laski, Marghanita, 181
Leavis, F.R., 60
Lee, London, 80–1, 94–8; Boone's chapel, 86; church of the Good Shepherd, 87–91, 94–8, 99–101, 173; St. Margaret's, 80–1, 85–6, 87
letters received, 149–150; *1955*, 164–9; from authors, 170–1; re depression, 207–8; re *Letters to Young Churches*, 109, 148–9; re *Ring of Truth*, 205–7
Lewis, C.S., 100, 107, 172; photo of, 158; royalties, 171–2
Limpley Stoke, conferences, 187–91
Living Church (Episcopalian U.S.A.), 109
London: suburbs, 11–12; *see also* Barnes; Blackheath; Lee; Penge; Wandsworth
London Bridge station, bomb at, 99
Los Angeles, 129–30, 132, 136–9
Luke, Gospel According to, 166–7
Luther, Martin, 147
Lutterworth Press, 125–6

Macmillan, publishers, New York, 128–9, 139; and *1958* holiday, 179, 181–6; premises, 182; publicity campaign, 179, 182
Manchester, Vermont, U.S.A., bookshop, 184
Mantle, Norman, 117, 128, 139
Mark, Gospel According to, 125; commentary, 212; translated, 168, 213
marriage, 85–6; divorce, 135
Marshall, Dr. Alfred, translation by, 166

Matthew, Gospel According to, 146, 192, 193
Mears, Henrietta, 131, 137
Meccano set, 32–3
Micah (prophet), 198, 199
Mojave Desert, California, 135
motor bike, 64
Moule, Professor Charles, 143, 190
Muir, Dr. Kathleen, 109, 110
music, 14–16, 61, 83–4
My Fair Lady (play), 183

Neville, John, 188
New English Bible, 191–3
New Testament: Authorised Version, 108, 141–2, 143–4, 146, 165; commentaries, 211–12; Epistles, 59, 94, 99–100; *see also names of recipients*; Gospels, 122–4, *see also names of Gospel writers*; Greek of, 141, 152; inspiration, 147–50; New English Bible, 191–3; translation, 94, 99–100, 117, 122–4, 150–3, 154–5, 165–8; *see also names of books*
New York, 128–9, 139, 177, 182, 183
New Zealand, letter from, 149
Norwood Cottage Hospital, 72–3, 74–6

Officers Training Corps, 50–1
Old Testament, 198–9
Olive (healer), 112–13
ordination, exam for, 70
Overstrand, Norfolk, 61–2
Oxford, 162

Paramount Film Studios, 137–9
Parker, Rev. W.P., 88
Pathfinder Press, 78
Paul, Saint, 152; idea of God, 167; style, 213; *see also* Epistles
Penfold, Rev. Murray, 163
Penge, London, 66, 67–72
perfectionism, 13–14, 16
Peter, Second Letter of, 147
Phillips, Dorothy Maud (sister of J.B.), 12, 15, 16, 45, 54, 55, 59, 60, 72, 186; in India, 71

Phillips, Emily Maud (mother of J.B.), 12, 14, 20, 31, 35; death, 37, 44
Phillips, Jennifer (daughter of J.B.), 158; birth, 109–10; in U.S.A., 128, 137–8; school, 155, 191; marriage, 109
Phillips, John Bertram: childhood, 9, 14–28, 29–43; parents, 12–13; schools, 14, 26–8, 31, 33, 36–7, 37–41, 43, 44, 45, 50–1; adolescence, 44–53, 54–66; University, 51–3, 55–8, 60–1, 62, 64–6; teaching, 62–3; editor, 78; marriage, 82–6, 109, 118; ordained, 66, 70; as minister, 67–71, 80–1, 87–93, 94–107, 111–26, 127–8, 139–40; illness, 35–6, 71–7; in U.S.A., 128–39, 181–6; broadcasting, 114–16, 124, 125, 126, 160–1, 177–8; translating, 122–4, 141–53, 173–4, 178–9, 212–13; in Swanage, 154–63; depression, 193–4, 196–7, 200–5, 207–11, 213–14; sales of books, 179: *The Church Under the Cross*, 171; *Four Prophets*, 194, 198–200; *The Gospels in Modern English*, 166; *Is God at Home?* 125–6; *Letters to Young Churches*, 100, 107–9, 116, 149; *Making Men Whole*, 171; *A Man Called Jesus*, 177–8; *New Testament Christianity*, 128, 172–3; *The New Testament in Modern English*, 178–9, 182, 184, 211–13; *Peter's Portrait of Jesus*, 212; *Ring of Truth*, 168, 205–7; *When God was Man*, 161; *The Young Church in Action*, 126, 157, 158–9; *Your God is Too Small*, 124–5
Phillips, Kenneth Charles (brother of J.B.), 12, 15, 16, 45, 58–9, 60, 158; career and death, 164
Phillips, Philip William (father of J.B.), 14, 16, 17–18, 19–21, 30, 34, 38, 42, 51, 76; and first wife, 12, 44; character and career, 13; religion, 24; second marriage, 44, 54; effect of image of, 77, 208

Phillips, Vera (née Jones: wife of J.B.), 88, 89, 90, 95–6, 128, 133, 140, 143, 154, 155, 156, 161, 162–3, 176–7, 186, 191, 200, 208; meets J.B., 82, 83–5; marriage, 85–6, 109, 118; as secretary, 194, 198
Picture Post, 120
plays, for B.B.C., 177–8
prayer: answered, 61–2; extempore, 131; and healing, 70, 112–14
Prayer, Book of Common, 24–5, 174
psychiatric treatment, 77, 202
Purcell, William, 115, 188, 189

Queen Elizabeth (liner), 128, 139
Queen Mary (liner), 181–2

Railway, London and South Western, 41–2
Redhill, Surrey; hospital, 118–19; St. John's, 100–7, 111–13, 117–22, 125, 127–8, 139–40; school, 103, 121–2
Reid, James, 81
Revelation of John, The, 173–4
Richmond Park, London, 30, 31, 50
Ridley Hall, Cambridge, 64–6
Rieu, Dr. E.V., 124, 151–2
Robertson, Edwin, 188, 194, 195, 198; at B.B.C., 115, 124, 126, 181; and commentaries, 211, 212; edits *The Price of Success*, 7
Robie, Col. John, 175, 177
Robinson, John, *Honest to God*, 205, 206–7
Romans, Letter of Paul to The, 143–4
Royal Air Force: in Battle of Britain, 88–9, 98; mission to, 126
Royal Earlswood Institution, Surrey, 103
Royal Naval station, Culdrose, 180–1
royalties, giving away, 171–2

St. Anton, house party, 78–9
St. Julian's, Sussex, retreat, 115
Salcombe, Devon, 34

Salisbury, 200; theological college, 195
Santa Barbara, California, 134 5
Schonfield, Hugh J., *The Passover Plot*, 205, 206
Scotland, 179–80
scout movement, 63, 68–9
sensitivity, 16
Shanklin, Isle of Wight, 34
Sheffield, 163–4
Sheppard, J. T., 58
Sherborne, Dorset, 163; Abbey, 162; Girls' School, 191; Prep School, 63–4
Sheils, Rev. D. A. P., 103
Simpson, Dr. B. F., 100–1
Simpson, Pat, 117, 128, 139
Sinclair, Pamela, 178
Skinner, David, 188
'spare', meaning of, 143–4
speak, requests to, 168–9
sports, 40 1, 57
Steele, Rev. Louis, 88
Stepmother, 44, 54
Stewart, James, 138
Stuart-Smith, T. G., 65
Student Christian Movement, 52
suburbs, London, 11–12
success, dangers of, 7–8, 29
suffering, problem of, 37, 113, 208–9, 213–14; *see also* depression
Swanage, Dorset: house party, 1935, 78–9; house built, 127, 128, 154, 155; life in, 1955, 154–7, 162; Wolfeton Hotel, 154
Sydenham, London, 164

Tatlock, Richard, 115
Taylor, Cyril, 115, 125
teaching, 63–4
telepathy, 119, 120; E.S.P., 71, 132–3
television, 161
Ten Commandments, The (film), 138
Timothy, Letters of Paul to, 193
Tonbridge, Kent, 98
translation: aims of, 123, 141, 150–1; faulty, examples of, 151–2, 165, 192–3;

translation – *cont.*
  fundamentalism and, 145–7;
  method, 141–3; of New
  Testament, 94, 99–100, 117,
  122–4, 150–3, 154–5; letters
  concerning, 165–8; at school, 51;
  New English Bible, 191–3
Trevelyan, Katharine, 116
Trotter, Miss (school teacher), 155
'Trout, Father', 58–60, 64, 145

U.S.A.: letters from, 109, 164–5;
  1954 tour, 127, 128–39; *1958*
  holiday, 179, 181–6; visitors from
  162–3
U.S. Air Force, mission to, 175–7
Urchfont Manor, near Devizes, 181

Vermont, U.S.A., 184–5
visiting: hospital, 118–19; parish,
  69–70

Walton, Robert, 177
Wandsworth, London S.E., 25–6, 33

Ward, R. H., 188, 189
Weekley, Dr. Edwin Thornton, 72,
  186
Whitmarsh, Gerald, 190, 194, 200
Williams, Harry, 209–10
Williams, Rev. John, 114
Willson, Martin: at B.B.C., 115, 160,
  191; Limpley Stoke conferences,
  187, 191; death, 191
wireless, 46–50, 66; press, 47
Woking, Surrey, 164
Woldingham, Surrey, 54, 58
women, attitudes to, 82–3
Woods, E. S., 55
World Association for Christian
  Communication, 195
World War I, 29, 30, 31, 38–9
World War II, 87, 88–93, 95–9,
  102–4
writing, copper-plate, 27

Yanovsky, Miss, 188, 190

Zeppelins, 30